TURKEY,
THE BEAST AND
THE COMING CALIPHATE

THE EMPIRE OF
ANTICHRIST

FOR THE TIME IS NEAR. - REVELATION 1:3

TIM BUCK

FOCUS
ON THE END TIMES
FOTET.ORG

The Empire of Antichrist: For the Time is Near

© Copyright 2021 by Tim Buck

ISBN: 978-1-63073-366-7

Faithful Life Publishers
North Fort Myers, FL 33903

FaithfulLifePublishers.com
888.720.0950

All Scripture quotations are taken from the New King James Bible.

Published in the United States of America

24 23 22 21   1 2 3 4 5

To the friends and partners of
Focus On The End Times Ministry
who long for the coming of our Lord Jesus Christ
and live with the hope of His soon return
burning in your heart. The Lord is soon coming
down, so keep on looking up.

Contents

Introduction

PINPOINTING THE EMPIRE OF ANTICHRIST

Little children, it is the last hour; and as you have heard that the Antichrist is coming, even now many antichrists have come, by which we know that it is the last hour.

1 John 2:18

The Antichrist generates a lot of interest among Christians and non-Christians alike, and in the above verse, the Apostle John makes it clear he is coming by contrasting the many antichrists in the world (lower case a) with the Antichrist (capital A).

The spirit of antichrist, which is at work in our world today, will one day be concentrated in one evil person.

The question is, when will he arrive? What are the signs of his coming? And can Bible prophecy help us pinpoint his coming more precisely?

To answer these questions, here are a few details about events that need to happen before Antichrist rises. The Bible is quite clear on how and when he arrives, with the book of

Daniel giving us the key sign that an empire precedes his arrival. This study helps to identify that empire.

Prophecy watchers often miss this point, assuming Antichrist will just appear out of the blue without any warning and that somehow, we will wake up some morning with Antichrist in control of the world! Many prophecy teachers today miss the *"elephant in the room"* prophecy that an empire precedes Antichrist's arrival on the world stage. That is a big miss! According to both the books of Daniel and Revelation, Antichrist will not appear until after Satan's eighth and final empire arrives. And that empire is not here yet.

To get us started pinpointing it, we need some background help from the Prophet Daniel.

Chapter 1

DANIEL, MAN GREATLY LOVED

When the angel Gabriel appeared to the Prophet Daniel, after he had been fasting and praying for three weeks (Daniel 10:2), the angel addressed the prophet by saying,

"O Daniel, man greatly loved, understand the words that I speak to you."

Daniel 10:11

Unless you have an angel appear to you like Daniel, it can be a struggle trying to understand the prophetic word. The reason for the struggle is because it is only possible through the illumination of the Holy Spirit. That illumination is what the church needs today. Despite the amount of scripture about these perilous times, there is confusion as to how it all fits together. My prayer is for this work to bring some clarity to help the church better understand the last days and the rising empire of Antichrist.

From the visions and dreams he received, the prophet Daniel reveals a great deal about the end times. So much so that the book of Daniel lays the foundation for understanding the book of Revelation. For instance, Daniel 9 contains the "70

Weeks" calendar that God revealed to Daniel about Israel's future (Daniel 9:24-27). The final seven years of that calendar remain unfulfilled, and the events are detailed in Revelation 6-19, known as the Tribulation Period. The idea of "beasts" being symbolic for empires first appears in Daniel 7 and is carried over into Revelation. All totaled, Revelation contains 34 direct references from the book of Daniel.

Daniel was a young man, maybe only 15 or 16 years old, when he made the 1000-mile journey from Israel to Babylon (Iraq). Though he didn't realize it then, young Daniel would spend 85 years away from his birthplace and while in Babylon, he would receive multiple prophesies to help us understand the last days.

DANIEL'S VISION OF ANTICHRIST AND JESUS CHRIST

There is little question that one of the most important portions of the Bible with regard to the subject of the end-times is the Book of Daniel. Its primary focus and emphasis is the final conflict between Antichrist, the followers of Antichrist and the people of God who are ultimately delivered by the coming of Jesus the Messiah-King. Virtually every chapter in Daniel deals with some element of this final clash.

Daniel addresses the geography from which Antichrist's empire will emerge, the timing of Antichrist's emergence, the nature of Antichrist's persecution against God's people, the religious motivations behind the aggressive wars of Antichrist, and the theology or belief system of Antichrist.

The Book of Daniel discusses the character, the perseverance, and the faith of God's people who become believers during the Tribulation period. Most importantly, his unique prophecy presents the ultimate victory of Jesus over Antichrist, followed by His glorious Messianic Kingdom.

Chapter 2

DANIEL'S PROPHECY DOES NOT INCLUDE ROME

THE FOURTH BEAST OF DANIEL 2 AND 7

In the prophecy of Daniel seven, Daniel sees four empires symbolically portrayed as beasts, beginning with his own empire, the Babylonian Empire. The symbolism of using beasts to represent empires which is first used by Daniel in chapter 7, is continued in the book of Revelation in chapters 13:1-2; 17:3, 8.

As we examine Daniel 7, we see a similar pattern of four beasts that begins back in Daniel 2. Although we are focusing here on Daniel 7, the same picture of four pagan empires is described in Daniel 2. The prophesies of both Daniel 2 and 7 describe four successive historical pagan empires, succeeded by one final last days empire. In Daniel 7, instead of using the imagery of a metallic statue as in Daniel 2, the story is told through the symbolism of four beasts. Daniel's vision in chapter 7 is simply a recapitulation of Nebuchadnezzar's dream in chapter 2.

Daniel explains the fourth empire would be revived in the last days and appear in the form of ten kings or ten nations (Daniel 7:24). He then explains that once the ten-kings form their empire, another king (Antichrist) will rise up from among the ten nations. This important sequence of the 10-king empire preceding the arrival of Antichrist is often overlooked but is a critical point for prophecy watchers today.

Satan's final empire of 10-kings will be firmly in place before the world gets its first glimpse of Antichrist. Most students of prophecy assume Antichrist can appear at any time. But that's incorrect. Daniel's sequence requires the establishment of the empire first. So it would be wise for students of prophecy to stop looking for Antichrist and start looking for the signs of the coming empire. If we correctly identify Daniel's fourth empire, it will show us more precisely where Antichrist will come from.

SHIFTING FROM EUROPEAN TO MIDDLE EASTERN PARADIGM

The identification of Daniel's fourth empire has been debated with interpreters suggesting it points to the Vatican, Russia, America, with the most popular view suggesting it points to the ancient Roman Empire. Unfortunately, these suggestions miss the mark by misunderstanding the sequence of Satan's seven empires outlined in Revelation 17:9-11 (which will be discussed later) and therefore leave out the most consistent Scriptural interpretation for Daniel's fourth empire as the revived Islamic Caliphate.

Consider that Daniel never mentions who the fourth beast is. Although the first three kingdoms in Daniel 2 are clearly identified by name as Babylon, Medo-Persia and Greece, the fourth empire is never named. But despite the lack of name identification Daniel provides crucial clues to enable us to properly identify it.

In the study that follows, we will examine three pieces of evidence against the identification of the fourth empire in Daniel 2 and 7 as the Roman Empire and why the historical Islamic Caliphate does meet the Scriptural criteria. History records the Islamic Caliphate as having its beginnings with the conquests of Muhammad, roughly 500 AD, and finding its culmination in the Ottoman Empire, 1453-1913 AD.

THE GEOGRAPHY OF THE FOURTH KINGDOM

The first problem with the Roman identification of the fourth kingdom is that the Roman Empire does not meet the specific criteria of Daniel 2:40. This verse helps define the size of the fourth kingdom. The text specifically says that at the time of its rise, the fourth kingdom would crush all three of the other kingdoms:

> And the fourth kingdom shall be as strong as iron…
> and like iron that crushes, that kingdom will break in
> pieces and crush all the others.

Daniel 2:40

Later in Daniel 7, speaking of this same empire, we find a very similar description:

> Thus he said: 'As for the fourth beast, there shall be
> a fourth kingdom on earth, which shall be different
> from all the kingdoms, and it shall devour the whole
> earth, and trample it down, and break it to pieces.

Daniel 7:23

The fourth kingdom will break and shatter the previous three kingdoms. The three other kingdoms that would be trampled and crushed are Babylon, Medo-Persia and Greece. The text is clear that the fourth kingdom would "crush" or conquer all three of these empires. Simply stated, the first criterion the fourth empire must meet is that its boundaries must include all the geographic territory of the first three empires. The Roman empire never meets that description!

The meaning of the word "crush" refers to capturing the geographic territory of the three former empires. By examining maps of the ancient Roman Empire, it is clear that the Roman Empire only conquered roughly one-third of the regions controlled by Babylon, Medo-Persia and Greece. But roughly two-thirds of the regions controlled by these empires were left entirely untouched by the Roman Empire.

In fact, the Roman Empire never even reached the two Persian capital cities of Ecbatana and Persepolis. Consider the following modern equivalence: If an invading nation conquered Boston, but never came close to reaching New York or Washington D.C., it would hardly be accurate to say that such a nation "crushed" the United States. Neither would it be correct to say that the Roman Empire crushed the entirety of the Babylonian, Medo-Persian or Grecian Empires. Yet the text is clear; in order to fulfill the criterion of Daniel 2:40, an empire would need to crush, not one, but all three of these. The Roman Empire simply does not fulfill this requirement.

Although the Roman Empire did conquer portions of the land holdings of the other empires, it clearly did not conquer all of them, not even a majority of them. The Roman Empire only conquered roughly 1/5 of the landholdings of the Medo-Persian Empire, whose capital cities of Ecbatana and Persepolis forever remained hundreds of miles out of the Roman Empire's reach. If we are to be honest, to say the Roman Empire fulfilled the criterion of Daniel 2:40 would be a stretch at best. On the other hand, the historical Islamic Caliphate fully, absolutely, and completely conquered all of the lands of the first three empires.

GRINDING THE CONQUERED TO DUST

The second problem for the Roman identification of the fourth empire is the criterion of Daniel 7:7, 19, 23. This time, instead of the size of the fourth kingdom, these verses speak of its reputation for crushing those it conquered until nothing was left but dust.

The vivid description in these verses makes it very difficult to be fulfilled by the Roman Empire when it says.

> Then I wished to know the truth about the fourth beast, which was different from all the others, exceedingly dreadful, with its teeth of iron and its nails of bronze, which devoured, broke in pieces, and trampled the residue with its feet.

> Daniel 7:19

The depiction here is of an overwhelming ferocious beast stomping up and down on its victims until nothing is left but dust. Quite an alarming picture! The question is, which one of the two choices, Rome or Islam, is the best match for this description? Remember, this isn't a meaningless portrayal but a solid clue that's repeated three times in the text. What it tells us is that when the fourth empire arrives, we will be able to recognize it by its reputation for annihilating everything it conquered. So much so that it would "break in pieces and trample the residue" of its foes "with its feet" into dust so there is nothing left.

Historians are quick to point out that the devastation of its subjects was not something Rome was known for, let alone its most prominent characteristic as stated in the text. However, the massacre and destruction of its subjects is precisely what the Islamic Empire practiced.

Rather than being a destructive force, Rome was a constructive force often adding infrastructure, order, and law to the lands it conquered even rebuilding Israel's temple in the time of Christ, which became known as 'Herod's Temple.' During a Passover visit by Jesus the Jews replied that their temple had been under construction for 46 years (John 2:20).

Rome was a nation-building empire that kept cultures, cities and languages intact and incorporated them into the Roman empire to increase their base for taxation.

The Islamic Empire had no such interests and from its inception was an Arab-Islamic-supremacist force that crushed and erased cultures and religions of the peoples it conquered.

For almost 500 years, from its defeat of the Roman Byzantine Empire in 1453, until its defeat in WW1 in 1913, the Turkish-led Ottoman Empire conquered and ruled by the sword. Its reputation for plundering, stealing, raping, destroying, and capturing its subjects is without equal.

This is due to the all-encompassing ideology of Islam, which includes every facet of life under Shariah law. Islam has rules and commandments that pertain to far more than just theology. It also dictates law, government, language, military, and even music, art, sexual and hygienic practices to those under its authority.

Islam is the epitome of a totalitarian ideology and wherever it spread, it brought its oppressive ideology of submission.

As an imperial force, Islam imposed its religion, culture, and language onto all its dominated peoples while erasing evidence of previous religions and non-Islamic cultures.

A modern example of the crushing spirit of Jihad is how the ISIS caliphate destroyed Syrian and Iraqi towns and people and demolished everything in their path including the region's ancient heritage sites.

Just as Daniel described, in the wake of the Islamic Caliphate, there is nothing left of former civilizations from the "trampling and stomping" but dust. So we see that Daniel's description of the fourth empire fails to match up to the Roman Empire. However, the Islamic Caliphate absolutely crushed all of the Babylonian, Medo-Persian, and Greek Empires. Beyond conquering their territories they successfully imposed their culture (Arab), their religion (Islam) and their language (Arabic) wherever they went. Thus we can conclude that the Islamic empire perfectly aligns with Daniel's description of the fourth empire.

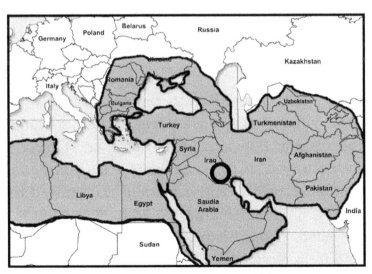

Islamic Caliphate (632-1923)

THE SECOND COMING WILL DESTROY THE FIRST 3 EMPIRES

The third problem for the Roman identification of the fourth empire is the criteria of Daniel 2:34-35. This time, instead of the size of the empire or its reputation for crushing its foes, these verses speak of its demise—the day of its destruction. This text speaks of the return of the Messiah Jesus and His kingdom. His kingdom is described as "a rock cut out, but not with human hands."

The Messianic Kingdom specifically destroys the final kingdom of Antichrist. But in doing so, we see that by virtue of the destruction of Antichrist's kingdom, Babylon, Medo-Persia and Greece are also all destroyed "at the same time."

> While you were watching, a rock was cut out, but not by human hands. It struck the statue on its feet of iron and clay and smashed them. Then the iron, the clay, the bronze, the silver and the gold were broken to pieces at the same time and became like chaff on a threshing floor in the summer. The wind swept them away without leaving a trace.
>
> Daniel 2:34-35

Simply stated, if the Roman Empire were fully revived today to the point of its greatest extent, and Jesus returned and fully destroyed it, Babylon, Medo-Persia and Greece would not all be destroyed "at the same time." Although a portion of the land holdings of these empires would be destroyed, roughly two-thirds of all three empires would be left untouched. On the other hand, if the Islamic Caliphate were fully revived today, and Jesus returned and conquered this empire, Babylon, Medo-Persia and Greece would by virtue all be completely destroyed as well. Once again, the Islamic Caliphate fulfills the criteria and requirements of the text, while the Roman Empire does not.

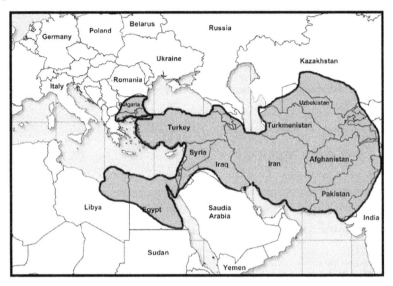

A combined Babylonian, Medo-Persian and Grecian Empire

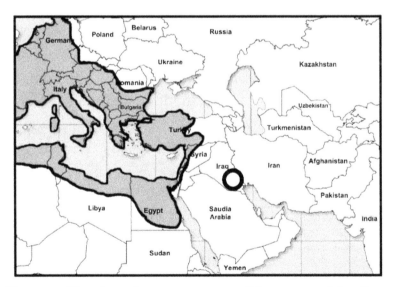

Roman Empire does not resemble a combination of Babylon (lion), Medo-Persian (Bear) and Greece (Leopard)

WESTERN VERSUS MIDDLE EASTERN CONTEXT

Despite the evidence we've considered, Westerners continue to struggle with the idea that the prophecy does not speak of the Roman Empire. Westerners struggle to recognize that the Babylonian through Roman interpretation is ultimately only true through the Western perspective and lens of history. Because Western culture traces its history and much of its culture through the Roman and Greek empires, Westerners tend to naturally assume that the Bible also views history from a Western perspective.

The context of this passage is a dream that was specifically given to Nebuchadnezzar, the King of Mesopotamia, concerning the kingdoms that would succeed his kingdom. This passage was revealed in Babylon, to a Babylonian King concerning kingdoms that would succeed his. This is seen clearly in the text.

> You, O king, are a king of kings... you are this head of gold. But after you shall arise another kingdom inferior to yours; then another, a third kingdom of bronze... And the fourth kingdom shall be as strong as iron...
>
> Daniel 2:37-39

The dream was not intended to reveal the future of America or the future of Europe. Instead, the dream was simply showing Nebuchadnezzar those kingdoms that would succeed his.

The First Four Empires of Daniel 2 and 7

1. Head of gold: Babylonian Empire

2. Chest and arms of silver: Medo-Persian Empire

3. Belly and thighs of bronze: Grecian Empire

4. Legs of iron: Islamic Caliphate

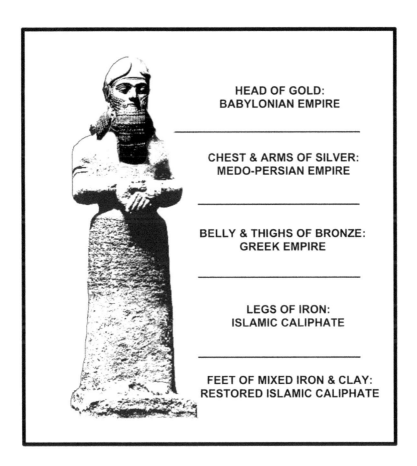

HEAD OF GOLD:
BABYLONIAN EMPIRE

CHEST & ARMS OF SILVER:
MEDO-PERSIAN EMPIRE

BELLY & THIGHS OF BRONZE:
GREEK EMPIRE

LEGS OF IRON:
ISLAMIC CALIPHATE

FEET OF MIXED IRON & CLAY:
RESTORED ISLAMIC CALIPHATE

SKIPPING ROME?

In suggesting the above understanding of Nebuchadnezzar's dream, many are skeptical that the Roman Empire is not included in the vision, yet no one has ever had any difficulty with the fact that the Parthian and Sassanid Empires are not included. This is despite the fact that the Parthian Empire ruled the region for well over a hundred years before the birth of the Roman Empire in Europe. But when we begin by acknowledging the Babylonian context of the dream, then the absence of Rome makes complete sense.

As we have already seen, while the Islamic Caliphate did completely conquer the entire region of ancient Babylon, as well as all of the former landholdings of Medo-Persia and Greece, the Roman Empire did not conquer all these regions. When we compare maps of Medo-Persia or Greece to a map of the Roman Empire, it becomes quite clear that the dominion of the Roman Empire was significantly more westward. The Roman Empire does not align itself to the context of the dream and was thus not included.

So now that we have identified Daniel's fourth beast as the Islamic Caliphate, it will help us pinpoint the area where its final day version will come from and the geography where Antichrist will appear.

Chapter 3

10 TOES, 10 HORNS, 10 KINGS, AND A CALIPHATE

It had huge iron teeth; it was devouring, breaking in pieces, and trampling the residue with its feet. It was different from all the beasts that were before it, and it had ten horns.

Daniel 7:7

The ten horns are ten kings who shall arise from this kingdom. And another shall rise after them; He shall be different from the first ones, and shall subdue three kings.

Daniel 7:24

10 HORNS REPRESENT THE REVIVAL OF THE FOURTH EMPIRE

According to Daniel's prophecy, out of the fourth empire grow ten horns. The ten horns represent the revived Ottoman Empire and correlate to the ten kings that make up Antichrist's empire, "The ten horns are ten kings who will arise from this kingdom."

The last-days ten kings are a prominent theme in Bible prophecy. The 10 kings are symbolically seen running through Daniel and Revelation as ten toes, ten horns and ten kings. The 10 kings are mentioned or alluded to a dozen times (Daniel 2:42, 44; 7:7, 24; 12:3; 13:1; 17:3, 12, 16-18).

According to Revelation 13:2, ten Muslim, Middle East nations form a final empire within the combined territory of Daniel's first 3 empires (Babylon (lion), Medo-Persian (Bear) and Grecian empires (Leopard). This means if we're looking for the empire to appear, we should focus on the Middle East not Russia, Europe, China, or America. The Apostle John uses the same symbolic beasts for the first three empires of Daniel 7 to describe the territory that will make up the empire of Antichrist.

> Now the beast which I saw was like a leopard (area of the Grecian empire), his feet were like the feet of a bear (area of the Medo-Persian empire), and his mouth was like the mouth of a lion (area of the Babylonian empire). The dragon gave him his power, his throne, and great authority.

> Revelation 13:2

The rise of 10-kings in the area of these former 3 empires is essential to be watching for. The urgency of this development is because the rise of the empire must occur BEFORE the start of the Tribulation. When considering a last-days prophetic timeline, this simple pre-tribulation sequence is important and goes like this: Once the empire of 10-kings is in place then the 11th king, Antichrist, will rise up from among the 10 kings. After Antichrist gains control of the empire he ascends to the vaunted position of "Caliph," the supreme ruler of the

Caliphate. Now controlling 10 oil-rich countries with nuclear powered militaries and in an enormously powerful position, he is able to turn his attention to making peace with Israel.

Through negotiations, Antichrist and Israel will agree upon a 7-year timeframe for Israel to divide her precious land into two states. Israel's gross mistake of dividing her promised land for an Allah worshipping, radical Muslim State and signing the 7-year agreement is what prompts God's wrath and triggers the start of the 7-year Tribulation (Daniel 9:27). The sequence and roll-out of all these events can unfold rather quickly.

It's very possible that within this decade we will see the dragon Satan begin to draw 10 Muslim kings together with the seductive opportunity and honor they won't be able to resist. His deceptions will overwhelmingly cause them to consider it to be the highest honor to serve Allah in this once-in-a-lifetime privilege of reviving the Islamic Empire. He will convince the 10-kings that the high calling of the mission is what all Muslims have been longing for since the Ottoman Caliphate was abolished by the allies after WWI in 1923.

The arrival of the 10-king Caliphate is one of the most important missing ingredients, yet to develop, that is necessary to launch the 7-year Tribulation. It is a vital piece of the end-time puzzle that must soon appear. The goal of a worldwide caliphate is central to the teaching of Islam. A caliphate forms the state government under Sharia Law that rules Islam. For almost 100 years, Muslims have been praying and waiting for the Caliphate to return and for Turkey to reestablish its leadership to guide and rule the religion of Islam.

The absence of a centralized government in Islam is comparable to Catholicism without the Vatican. This is a peril the Muslim world has unhappily endured now for almost one hundred years. How long can it continue without its government to guide the faith? Since Turkey was the last rightful head of the Caliphate and ruled it in grandeur with "great pomp and circumstance" for 500 years, she is looked upon more than any other nation including Saudi Arabia as the sole heir to revive it today.

As Westerners, it's difficult to imagine the euphoria surrounding an announcement of the arrival of the Islamic Empire! The excitement and anticipation will be over-the-top and the news will rock the Muslim world. Just as people from all over the world excitedly travelled to join ISIS, Muslims from all over the world will want to be part of this revived Ottoman Caliphate.

> So they worshiped the dragon (Satan/Allah) who gave authority to the beast (Caliphate); and they worshiped the beast, saying, "Who *is* like the beast? Who is able to make war with him?"

> Revelation 13:4

Throughout the book of Revelation the 'Caliphate-Beast' continuously blasphemes God, especially the deity and honor of Jesus Christ as the Son of God (1 John 2:22; Revelation 13:5-6; 17:3). Such blasphemy comes from the Quran. Although difficult to understand, these events are arranged under the providence of God as declared in the verses below. Everything takes place for His purposes! Once the Turkish-led Caliphate returns it is destined as God's tool of judgment for this world.

> The 10 horns you saw are 10 kings… These are of one mind and give their power and authority to become the beast (Caliphate)… For God has put it into their

hearts to fulfill His purpose, to be of one mind and give their kingdom to the beast.

Revelation 17:12-17

The above passage gives an apt description of the Caliphate explaining that the 10 kings become a single empire. Saying, *"they give their authority to the beast"* is expressing the notion the ten have surrendered their independent autonomy for the one purpose of *"giving their kingdom to the beast (Caliphate)."* Thus each king will choose to dissolve their independent country and amalgamate them into a single empire to become part of what they feel is a much bigger cause than just being king of a single nation.

Accepting this challenge will be the most crucial decision the 10-kings ever make. This is a do or die mission and they are aware of the consequences. According to Shariah law, once the Caliphate is commenced, the caliph or leader must always be in a state of conquering (Jihad) or he is in jeopardy of forcefully being removed. Planning *jihad* and imperial expansion becomes the moral duty and mission of the Caliphate. This is expressed in the wording of the First Seal Judgment of Revelation when Antichrist rides out on his white horse. Notice the phrase describing his mission.

And its rider had a bow, and a crown was given to him, and he came out conquering, and to conquer.

Revelation 6:2

The verse doesn't say Antichrist is going out to war or even going to battle. Instead, the text precisely describes his purpose as *"going out conquering"* which is the modus operandi of the caliph whose purpose is to always be expanding the empire with the ultimate mission of "conquering" the whole world.

This is what sets the "Beast" apart and makes the final empire so dangerous. And this is why Antichrist is so reckless. They are on a demonically empowered course of conquering the nations for Allah. The initial thrust of the beast will be to set its sights on the Muslim nations that are not yet part of the ten-king Caliphate. As that path develops they will take aim at the non-Muslim countries. When considering the potential of a nuclear-powered Caliphate the death toll will be incalculable.

> Their slain will be left unburied, and the stench of their corpses will rise; the mountains will flow with their blood.
>
> Isaiah 34:3

> Declare that this is what the LORD says: The corpses of men will fall like dung upon the open field, like newly cut grain behind the reaper, with no one to gather it.
>
> Jeremiah 9:22

In other words, the beast sets sail on a mission of death and once begun, there is no looking back. The decision to pull-the-trigger on launching such an enterprise involves not only the 10 kings but their governments, their families and all the people in their respective countries. By launching the Caliphate, the ten founding kings have set themselves apart to band together as the righteous followers of Allah. These are the Muslim 10-kings who are willing to risk it all.

Without realizing it, the 10-kings have been fully deceived by Satan who is Allah and will be used by the enemy to fight against the Lord (Revelation 19:19-20). As a result of their commitment, the beast will turn into such a deadly force that

Jesus warned it would wipe out earth's population if he didn't intervene to prevent it.

> For then there will be great distress, unequaled from the beginning of the world until now and never to be equaled again.

> If those days had not been cut short, no one would survive, but for the sake of the elect (Israel) those days will be shortened.

Mt. 24:21-22

It should be understood that the number ten representing these kings is not a symbolic number and should be taken literally because God repeats or alludes to the ten so frequently in Daniel and Revelation.

10 TOES, 10 HORNS, 10 KINGS		
SYMBOL	**TEXT**	**MEANING**
10 Toes	Dan. 2:42	10 toes represent the final empire on Daniel's Image
10 Kings	Dan. 2:44	The 10 toes represent the 10 future kings
10 Horns	Dan. 7:7	10 horns appear on the fourth beast in Daniel's vision of empires
10 Horns	Dan. 7:24	The 10 horns are 10 future kings

10 TOES, 10 HORNS, 10 KINGS		
SYMBOL	**TEXT**	**MEANING**
10 Horns	Rev. 12:3	10 horns appear on Satan's head showing that he empowers the 10-King Empire
10 Horns	Rev. 13:1	10 horns appear on the Beast, the 8th Empire, showing it's a 10-King Empire
10 Horns	Rev. 17:3	10 horns appear on the Scarlet Beast, showing it's a 10-King Empire
10 Horns	Rev. 17:12	The 10 horns represent 10 kings
10 Horns	Rev. 17:16-18	10 kings surrender authority to the Beast to become the revived Ottoman Caliphate

From the above chart we learn that the ten kings refer to ten contemporary kings reigning at the same time. They are not somehow representative of ten regions of the world as is sometimes thought. We see they are 10 ruling kings because they are still reigning together when Christ returns and defeats them at His Second Coming.

The (10) toes of the feet were partly of iron and partly of clay. And in the days of these (10) kings the God of heaven will set up a kingdom which shall never be destroyed; and the kingdom shall not be left to other people; it shall break in pieces and consume all these kingdoms, and it shall stand forever.

Daniel 2:42, 44

If we are now living under the shadow of the Tribulation as so many prophecy teachers including myself believe we are, then the rise of this empire must already be underway. Even more important to keep in mind is the fact that almost certainly by now, Satan precisely knows the name and location of each of the 10- kings, as well as Antichrist and has already been maneuvering them into position.

In order for the events of the Tribulation to explode onto the world when Antichrist signs the peace agreement with Israel, the 10-king empire must already be inaugurated. This is illustrated by the fact that when the Lamb of God opens the first seal in heaven (Revelation 6:1), Antichrist comes charging out on his white horse and immediately begins conquering. Therefore, if he's ready to ride forth at the start of the Tribulation, like a sprinter at the sound of the gun, the events of the rising Caliphate and Antichrist's ascension to the position of Caliph (ruler of the Caliphate) must happen long before then… and therefore must be underway today!

Now I saw when the Lamb opened one of the seals; and I heard one of the four living creatures saying with a voice like thunder, "Come and see." And I looked, and behold, a white horse. He who sat on it had a bow; and a crown was given to him, and he went out conquering and to conquer.

Revelation 6:1-2

THE LITTLE HORN IS ANTICHRIST

> I was considering the horns, and there was another horn, a little one, coming up among them, before whom three of the first horns were plucked out by the roots. And there, in this horn, were eyes like the eyes of a man, and a mouth speaking pompous words.
>
> Daniel 7:8

As Daniel watches his vision unfold, he notices another horn rising up among the ten horns. This is an important clue about Antichrist that is often missed. Not only does Antichrist arrive after the empire, but he comes out of the empire. Or said another way, the revived Ottoman Caliphate will give birth to Antichrist. This means Antichrist will come out of one of the ten Muslim nations forming the Caliphate. If we are looking for Antichrist to appear from Rome, Brussels, Moscow, Washington DC or Jerusalem we are looking in the wrong location.

Daniel then describes Antichrist as the "little horn" that uproots three of the ten horns and takes charge over the ten. Here we are introduced to Antichrist, the leader of the final kingdom.

Daniel is so amazed by what he sees concerning this fourth beast and the little horn, that he appeals twice to his interpreting angel (vs. 15-16, 19) to help him try to better understand what they mean.

> Then I wished to know the truth about the fourth beast, which was different from all the others, exceedingly dreadful, with its teeth of iron and its nails of bronze, which devoured, broke in pieces, and trampled the residue with its feet; and the ten horns

that were on its head, and the other horn which came up, before which three fell, namely, that horn which had eyes and a mouth which spoke blasphemous words, whose appearance was greater than his fellows.

I was watching; and the same horn was making war against the saints, and prevailing against them, until the Ancient of Days came, and a judgment was made in favor of the saints of the Most High, and the time came for the saints to possess the kingdom.

Daniel 7:19-22

The "little horn" represents Antichrist who John says keeps running his mouth and speaking blasphemous words and who pursues persecuting God's people. This scene is very much in line with what we would anticipate from the leader of the Islamic Caliphate who follows the Quran. The actions most emphasized throughout Daniel 7 about Antichrist are his arrogant and blasphemous words against the Lord. Daniel's comments about the evil nature and blasphemy of Antichrist stems from the fact that five times a day, Muslims repeat the blasphemous Shahada prayer saying, "there is no god but Allah." As Daniel points out, this is a direct assault on God Almighty, "the Most High."

As we've seen throughout chapter 7, Daniel reiterates the information one final time:

The ten horns are ten kings who shall arise from this kingdom. And another shall rise after them; He shall be different from the first ones and subdue three kings. He shall speak pompous words against the Most High, Shall persecute the saints of the Most High, and shall intend to change times and law. Then the saints shall be given into his hand for a time and times and half a time.

Daniel 7:24-25

Chapter 4

THE TURKS ARE COMING

In Daniel's vision we determined the ten kings represent the revived Ottoman Caliphate that will rise before the appearance of Antichrist. This means that even before the Rapture, and certainly before the seven-year Tribulation, we should begin to see the rise of Turkey, the former head of the Ottoman Empire. The transformation of Turkey and its quest for the rebirth of the Ottoman Empire is one the most important signs to be watching for today.

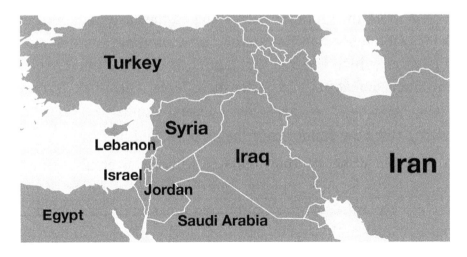

There are specific prophesied events that must happen before anyone gets their first glimpse of Antichrist. Could he be alive today? Most certainly. The length of time for these things to play out may only be a few years once the prophesied empire is formed. The groundwork for the rebirth of the Ottoman Empire has been developing for twenty years inside of Turkey, spearheaded by its Islamist president, Recep Tayyip Erdogan.

THE TRANSFORMATION OF TURKEY

Aside from Israel, Turkey is the most important nation to be watching relative to Bible prophecy.

Since Turkey was the head of the former Ottoman Empire, this indicates that Turkey's "head wound" described in Revelation (13:3), should be healing as we approach the Tribulation. Put another way, if the Ottoman Empire is to revive again in fulfillment of Daniel's prophecy of the fourth beast, then by now, its transformation should be in full swing and nearing completion.

In 1453, the Ottoman Turks sacked the eastern capitol of the Byzantine Roman Empire of Constantinople and renamed it Istanbul which became the capitol of the Ottoman Empire until their defeat in 1923. After their defeat, the allies' Sykes-Picot Agreement divided the Ottoman lands creating the twenty-two new countries of the modern Middle East.

In the wake of their defeat, Mustafa Kemal Ataturk established a secular republic and dissolved the office of the Caliph. The office of the Caliph combines political, military, and spiritual authority in one man and will be resumed by Antichrist.

According to their new secular constitution Turkey was forbidden to re-establish a Caliphate as the governing authority of the Islamic world and if the country ever drifted back into Islamism, the Turkish military was the constitutionally empowered guardian to prevent it.

For eighty years Turkey was regarded by the West as the model for the future of the Middle East where a moderate form of Islam coexisted with a modern secular state. As the eastern anchor of NATO, Turkey played a key role in the US and European defence strategy.

ARRIVAL OF ISLAMIST PRESIDENT ERDOGAN

That all changed with the rise of Islamist President Recep Tayyip Erdogan in 2001 and the establishment of his Justice and Development Party (AKP) in Turkey.

Erdogan's Islamist movement in Turkey has stunned the world and prophecy watchers alike. He has steadily undermined the secular legacy of its founder Kemal Ataturk by restoring pride in the outlawed Islamic Empire. This has been achieved through an aggressive mosque building campaign. Today, Turkey has some ninety-thousand mosques under the office of the Directorate of Religious Affairs (Diyanet) which employs 125,000. The Diyanet employs all of Turkey's Imams, organizes Quran courses for children, issues its interpretations of Islamic norms, and drafts sermons to be read in the country's mosques.

The Directorate also has thousands of mosques across Europe, Africa, Central and Southeast Asia and the United States. Several years ago they embarked on a "super mosque" building program erecting thirty-two massive mosques at home and abroad.

While busy building mosques, Erdogan has also been removing Christians at home, closing down churches, jailing pastors, shutting down Christian websites, and turning a blind eye to Islamic terror attacks that target Christians in Turkey.

In the once-secular Turkey, hate for Christians has, in fact, come to permeate every segment of society — from the average Muslim citizen to the highest levels of government. The examples of the persecution of Christians and attacks on their churches could fill a series of books.

One such example was committed by a group of five young Turks, including the son of a mayor, who broke into a Bible publishing house in Malatya. They bound and interrogated its three Christian employees, tortured them for hours, slit their throats and murdered them. "We didn't do this for ourselves, but for our religion," one of the accused Turks said.

SUPPORT FOR TERRORISTS, HATRED FOR CHRISTIANS

Erdogan's support for terrorists ranges from Al Qaeda to ISIS and Hamas, the Palestinian terror group to whom he funds $300 million a year. Erdogan recently gave citizenship to senior Hamas leaders, all designated terrorists by the U.S. State Department, whom he allows to reside in Turkey, making it easier for them to travel worldwide.

Across Turkey, anything Christian is under assault — people, buildings, churches, and even Christian cemeteries.

What is behind all the attacks on anything and everything Christian is described in a response of a journalist in Turkey as an "environment of hate."

> "The hateful environment did not emerge out of nowhere. The seeds of this hatred are spread, beginning at primary schools, through books printed by the Ministry of National Education portraying Christians as enemies and traitors. The indoctrination continues through newspapers and television channels in line with state policies. And of course, the sermons at mosques and talk at coffee houses further stir up this hatred."

In other words, Turks, once "secular," are now educated to hate Christians.

While building mosques and persecuting Christians, Erdogan lauds Turkey's Ottoman heritage from his presidential palace.

President Erdogan has built a 1,000 room, 3.1 million square foot palace for himself that cost the Turkish government $615 million dollars! Erdogan's palace is the most expensive palace in the world today!

As you might expect Turkish citizens as well as Turkish leaders have protested the costliness of Erdogan's palace. He responds by saying, "No one can prevent the completion of this building. If they are powerful enough, let them come and demolish it."

The palace is known as the "White Palace" and sits upon a hilltop overlooking Turkey's capital city of Ankara. The White Palace is bigger than the Whitehouse. It is bigger than the Kremlin. It is bigger than the palace of Versailles.

This is where President Erdogan now lives. Inside the palace, President Erdogan often has Turkish soldiers dress in the period correct armor of Ottoman Empire era military. By doing this, Erdogan openly honors the 500 years of conquests of the Ottoman Empire!

President Erdogan says that the palace symbolizes a resurgent Turkey. I think what he means to say is, "The palace is the future headquarters of the revived Ottoman Caliphate."

Whenever given the chance, Erdogan lashes out against Israel and threatens to rally the Muslim world to war against the Jewish State. Today, Erdogan is the most powerful voice in the Muslim world for the Palestinian people and is a strong influence among Palestinians living in Judea, Samaria (West Bank) and Gaza.

Some of that influence has come from the goodwill he's gained through projects like rebuilding the public utilities destroyed in Gaza after their conflicts with Israel, by pouring millions of dollars into East Jerusalem to help the poor and for new projects related to the Temple Mount where he seeks to gain more influence and control.

After a failed army led coup against him in July 2016, Erdogan used the fiasco to purge the government, military, police, the judiciary, education and media by arresting and jailing hundreds of thousands in a brutal crackdown.

In just 20 years, Erdogan has effectively brought an end to the secular republic established by Ataturk. He is now openly talking about his intention to reconstitute the Ottoman Empire and return Turkey to its former glory as the head of Islam.

RISING LEADER OF SUNNI ISLAM

President Erdogan has masterfully positioned himself as the leader of Sunni Islam, the majority sect of Islam. He is recognized by Sunni nations as wearing the mantle of the Islamic empire, and many of these nations would quickly endorse his movement to reestablish the Ottoman Caliphate.

And in a final area of interest for students of prophecy, Erdogan has led Turkey to ally with Muslim nations important to end-time prophecy like Libya, Sudan, Jordan, the Palestinians, and even nuclear powered Iran and Pakistan (Ezekiel 38:1-6; Daniel 11:41).

As we now live under the shadow of the Tribulation, Satan's final empire is forming. With the transformation of Turkey, President Erdogan or his successor is well positioned to form a coalition of Muslim nations just as Daniel saw twenty-five hundred years ago.

Whether this year or in ten years, the boiling pot of the Middle East is preparing to give birth to the prophesied "beast" spoken about in Daniel and Revelation, the revived Islamic Caliphate. The "beast" (Revelation 13:1; 17:16-17), consisting of ten Muslim nations, will become Satan's driving force of terror as well as God's weapon to inflict judgment in the seven-year Tribulation.

THE RETURN OF THE OTTOMAN CALIPHATE

There is plenty of evidence to believe Turkey is planning to re-launch the Ottoman Caliphate. Erdogan's state-run media, for its part, continue to promote the idea that Turkey is the natural protector of all Muslims. Since the coup in 2016,

Erdogan has indicated he would like to revive the Ottoman Caliphate by 2023 when Turkey celebrates its one-hundredth anniversary of becoming a republic.

By reviving the institution of the Caliphate, Turkey would claim the moral, political, spiritual, and religious leadership of the Muslim world giving Erdogan immense control and influence over Muslims around the globe.

The new Caliphate will become an imposing super-power overnight as the world wakes up to find ten Muslim nations have combined their oil and gas revenue, financial assets, military equipment, and armies into one unified empire. Whatever agreements the ten nations had with other countries will now vanish or need to be renegotiated through the office of the Caliph in Turkey.

One can only imagine the immediate impact of this on financial markets and the shifting of alliances across the world. How the United States, Europe and Israel react to the establishment of what could best be described as a nuclear-powered ISIS remains to be seen but scripture gives us a good picture of the fear generated by its presence,

> The world marveled and followed the beast... and they worshiped the beast, saying, Who is like the beast? Who is able to make war with him?

> Revelation 13:3-4

If President Erdogan is in power, he would likely be chosen as the first Caliph. If he is no longer in power, then his successor or another Sunni leader will be chosen to rule the new empire. The Caliph is the head of the Caliphate who was sometimes referred to as Sultan. It is a unique position and something like combining the Pope, the President of the

United States and a five-star general into one person. This creates a powerful position for just one man, and as Daniel points out, it is a role perfectly suited for Antichrist,

> Then the king shall do according to his own will: he shall exalt and magnify himself above every god, shall speak blasphemies against the God of gods, and shall prosper till the wrath has been accomplished; for what has been determined shall be done.
>
> Daniel 11:36

Erdogan has moved his country out of the western moderate camp into the Iranian radical camp. Iranian national policy seeks the "total annihilation" of Israel and so does Erdogan. And it's the city of Jerusalem that both Erdogan and the leaders of Iran now openly say they want to conquer. Just as indicated in the alliance of Ezekiel 38, Turkey and Iran are working together and laying the groundwork for Satan's final empire.

No one seems to be able to slow the pace of Turkey's rise in the region; not the US, Russia or the EU. Erdogan's tactic of releasing millions of Muslim refugees into Europe has sidelined the EU nations, who have become fearful of further Turkish retaliation. This has brought EU appeasement of Turkey's illegal activities on multiple fronts like its illegal gas and oil exploration in the eastern Mediterranean, its military incursion into Libya, and its push to expand their boundaries into northern Syria and Iraq to better match their former Ottoman territory.

TURKEY'S AGGRESSION ON THE RISE

The Turkish military is now engaged in wars of aggression in Libya, northern Syria, northern Iraq, Greece and Cyprus. According to prophecy, this is just the beginning. The mindset within the spirit of Islam that drives Antichrist is bent on regaining all the land once conquered by the Ottomans, then domination of the region followed by domination of the world!

Erdogan's anti-Israel rhetoric and determination to reestablish its Ottoman heritage is being orchestrated by Satan who seems to be pushing for reviving the Ottoman Caliphate this decade, marking the 100th anniversary of its demise – 2023-24. Until that empire rises, there will be no sign of Antichrist.

Now that we've discussed the movement inside Turkey to revive the Ottoman Caliphate let's look at the Biblical prophecies laying out the Islamic connection to both Antichrist and his empire.

Chapter 5

SEVEN DOWN AND ONE TO GO

Having concluded our study on the rise of Turkey, we now turn our attention to the subject of the 7-headed beast in Revelation. We will find that the story being told in the Book of Revelation is simply retelling the same story told in Daniel about another empire rising up opposing God and Israel in the last days. For our purposes, we will begin in Revelation 13. Like the rest of the Book of Revelation, the story is told using a strong dose of symbolism, but don't let that scare you. Once the symbolism is unraveled, the message will become quite clear.

FROM THE SEA OF GENTILE NATIONS SURROUNDING ISRAEL

No story, however wicked or perverse, imagined or real, can compare with the end-time scene the apostle John presents to his readers in Revelation 13. The star subject of the chapter is the beast who appears like nothing we've seen up to this point and symbolically represents the revived Ottoman Caliphate. We learn that the dragon (Satan) summons the beast "out of the sea" to carry out the final stage of Satan's strategy. The phrase, "out of the sea" is a reference to the Gentile nations

(Isaiah 60:5; Revelation 17:1, 15) and points to the Muslim countries surrounding Israel today.

> The dragon (Satan) stood on the shore of the sea. And I saw a beast rising up out of the sea (of nations), having seven heads and ten horns, and on his horns ten crowns, and on his heads was a blasphemous name.
>
> Revelation 13:1

BEAST: SYBOLIC MEANING FOR KINGDOM OR EMPIRE

First, we need to understand that this symbol of a "beast" represents a kingdom or an empire. The basis for this interpretation is found in Daniel 7 where Daniel saw four beasts, each one also arising from out of the sea. When the prophet Daniel asked an angel the meaning of the beasts, he was told they each represent a different empire (Daniel 7:23). So, in Revelation 13, as in Daniel 7, the beast represents a satanically empowered kingdom or empire that rises out of the sea of gentile (Muslim) nations surrounding Israel.

THE 7 HEADS REPRESENT 7 HISTORICAL EMPIRES

We next see that the beast is said to have seven heads. It is important to understand that these 7 heads symbolize 7 previous empires Satan used in seeking to destroy God's chosen people. The symbolism of the 7 heads is used 4 times in Revelation 12:3; 13:1 and 17:3, 7. Each time it is used, it symbolizes the 7 historic empires Satan has used throughout history to carry out his opposition to God and to either assimilate or annihilate the Jewish people. Since ancient Egypt in 1400 BC, Satan has had a successive string of empires in place that would be ready to either kill the coming Messiah when he arrives, or to persecute Israel and control Jerusalem.

What we learn from this picture is that these seven historical empires have essentially been the devil's puppets to carry out his work of resisting the Lord's unfolding plan of redemption. This is why it is said that Satan will bestow upon the beast "his power and his throne and great authority" (Rev. 13:2). Even as Satan has worked through these historical beast kingdoms, his greatest work will be carried out through the final kingdom of the beast.

Though there have been many satanically empowered empires and nations throughout history, the seven heads of the beast represent seven very specific empires through which Satan has sought to wage war against God's purposes. These are the primary empires that have at one time or another ruled over the promised land and most often have sought to destroy God's people.

While Daniel 7 gives us a partial picture revealing only four pagan kingdoms (Babylon, Medo-Persia, Greece, and the Ottoman Caliphate), Revelation 13 and 17 convey a much fuller picture, spanning all of Biblical history. So, which empires do the seven heads represent?

IDENTIFYING THE FIRST SIX EMPIRES

The first head of the beast represents the ancient pagan empire of Egypt. This is the Egypt of Pharaoh, which enslaved the Hebrews and chased them into the desert for extermination. This Egypt represented the first great satanic attack on God's chosen people, the Hebrews. The second pagan empire to assault God's people was Assyria, which, under Sennacherib, attacked and carried into exile the ten northern tribes of Israel. After this, it was Babylon, under Nebuchadnezzar, who attacked the southern kingdom of Judah, destroying Jerusalem and carrying the nation away into exile.

The fourth great pagan empire was Medo-Persia, from which came Haman and his devilish plot to exterminate the Jewish people, as recorded in the book of Esther. Then came the Greeks, led by Alexander the Great, who conquered the whole of the Middle East. After Alexander's death, it was through the Greek king Antiochus IV Epiphanes that Satan once more waged a horrific assault against the people of God.

The next satanically empowered kingdom, of course, was Rome, which oppressed and occupied the promised land during Jesus' day. It was under the Roman empire that Jesus was crucified. Forty years later, under Emperor Titus, Jerusalem and the temple would be destroyed and many of the citizens of the land killed or exiled. Up to this point, these are the first six empires:

FIRST SIX EMPIRES

1. Egyptian Empire

2. Assyrian Empire

3. Babylonian Empire

4. Medo-Persian Empire

5. Grecian Empire

6. Roman Empire

KEYS TO THE SEQUENCE OF THE SEVEN EMPIRES

Most commentators would agree with the names on this list. Not surprisingly, though, there is some controversy surrounding the identity of the beast's seventh head. Many interpreters suggest it represents a revived Roman empire led by Antichrist. There is a glaring problem with this view, however, because the seventh empire arrives AFTER Rome. And beyond the seventh empire, the angel went on to describe another mysterious eighth empire. What are we to make of this? Surely the eighth kingdom cannot be a double-revived Roman Empire. Rome cannot be the sixth, the seventh, and the eighth, can it?

Rome appearing three times wouldn't seem to make any sense and consistency requires that we see each head as a distinct empire. The eighth is the only exception, as it is linked to the one before it. The key, then, is to identify the seventh head first. The eighth is the revival of the seventh head. So what empire might this be? Which empire came after Rome and reigns before the 8th and final empire of Antichrist?

Based on scripture and the chronological narrative of history, it seems clear the seventh empire is the Ottoman Empire. The Ottoman Caliphate that ruled the Middle East for 500 years best fits the Biblical criteria of these four key factors essential for making that determination.

FACTORS TO DETERMINE THE SEVENTH EMPIRE

1. The Chronology of the Empires

The seventh kingdom had not yet risen to power in John's day. Since Rome was ruling at the time of John's writing, the potential candidates are restricted to the empires that ruled over the land of Israel and Jerusalem after the fall of the Roman Empire.

2. The Continuity of the Empires

The first six empires were successive, rising one after the other, without interruption. Egypt rose to power and was defeated by the Assyrians. In turn, Assyria fell to the Babylonians. The Babylonian empire was conquered by the Medo-Persians. The Medo-Persian Empire succumbed to the hand of Alexander the Great as the Grecian Empire rose to power.

The Greeks then fell to the Romans. Emperor Constantine moved the Roman capital to Byzantium (modern-day Istanbul, Turkey) and renamed it Constantinople. When the Ottoman Empire rose to power and conquered Constantinople, it brought the Roman Empire to an end. Thus it continued the successive line of uninterrupted empires in the same pattern with the first six empires.

3. The Natural Grouping of the First Seven Empires

Did you notice that in John's description (Revelation 17:10) he uses very few words when alluding to the seventh empire? He simply states, "the other has not yet come." It's as if he assumes his readers will understand the natural progression from the first six to the seventh empire. That's because he is grouping these first seven together due to their similar nature and their uninterrupted progression of one following the other. Satan has always had one of these empires on duty in succession for 4000 years from Egypt unto the end of WWI. The Ottoman Caliphate, as the seventh, fits neatly within the grouping of the previous six.

4. The Geographic Relationship of the First Seven Empires

The territorial areas controlled by the Islamic Ottoman Empire at the height of its power have a consistent geographic relationship with the previous six empires. Essentially, any empire outside of the geographic region of the Middle East would seem to be an unlikely candidate for the seventh empire. This feature is true even about the Roman empire. Its western division dissolved in 476 AD. However, 150 years before it dissolved, in 325 AD, the Emperor Constantine moved the Roman Capitol to Turkey. The eastern Roman Empire remained headquartered in Turkey for 1000 years until it was conquered by the Ottoman Empire in 1453 AD.

The only real candidate to fit all these factors as the seventh empire and the only empire that closely follows the clearly established pattern set by the previous six is the Ottoman Empire.

BIBLICAL MATH AND THE 7 HEADS OF REVELATION 17

Thankfully, the symbolism and meaning of the seven heads is specifically addressed in Revelation 17 where the same beast is again pictured. There we learn once again that the seven heads are seven kingdoms or empires. Interpreting these three verses is crucial to understanding the sequence of the seven empires:

> Here is the mind which has wisdom. The seven heads are seven mountains (Kingdoms) upon which the woman sits, and they are seven kings; five have fallen, one is, the other has not yet come; and when he comes (Antichrist), he must continue a short time. And the beast which was, and is not, is himself also an eighth and is *one* of the seven, and he goes to destruction.
>
> Revelation 17:9-11

SEVEN HEADS ARE SEVEN MOUNTAINS

Here we see the seven heads are called seven mountains. This has thrown some people off, but the symbolism of a mountain is commonly used to refer to a kingdom or empire (Ps. 30:7; 68:15-16; Isa. 2:2; 41:15; Jer. 51:25; Dan. 2:35; Hab. 3:6, 10; Zech. 4:17). When Christ returns at His Second Coming to establish His Millennial Kingdom, the prophet Daniel says the whole earth is filled with His mountain kingdom.

> Then the iron, the clay, the bronze, the silver, and the gold were crushed together, and became like chaff from the summer threshing floors; the wind carried them away so that no trace of them was found. And the stone that struck the image became a great mountain and filled the whole earth.
>
> Daniel 2:35, 45

The Book of Obadiah for instance, is entirely a prophecy concerning "the Mountain of Edom" in conflict with "Mount Zion." The prophecy is not literally speaking of a conflict between two mountains, rather two kingdoms: The Kingdom of Moab versus the Kingdom of Israel.

Some have seen this passage as referring to Rome thinking it relates to the ancient city sitting on seven "hills." But further examination reveals this to be a problematic position. The word used in this passage is not the Greek word for hills (*bounos*), but mountains (*oros*). If Rome were the subject of this passage, the author would have used the word for hills, not mountains. And even beyond this, we need to remember that this is an end-times passage. It is not speaking of an ancient reality. The city of Rome today sits on ten hills, not seven mountains.

Despite the popularity of this interpretation throughout the years, the idea that this passage is speaking about the city of Rome is untenable.

It is through a series of pagan world empires that Satan has waged his war against God and His people down throughout the ages. The seven-headed beast is the personification of Satan's activity in the earth. Even as the Church represents the Body of Christ, so also does the beast represent the Body of Satan.

Here in Revelation 17:9-11, with only a few chapters remaining before the end of the Bible, God chose to finally reveal the mathematical sequence and order of all seven empires. These are the only three verses in the Bible that present a complete overview of the seven empires and the only verses that tell us there will be a future eighth empire.

Once it is understood that the mountains are kingdoms, the passage is easy to understand.

MASTER LIST OF EIGHT EMPIRES

1. **Egypt**

2. **Assyria**

3. **Babylon**   }   **"FIVE HAVE FALLEN"**

4. **Persia**

5. **Greece**

—————————————

6. **Rome**   }   **"ONE IS" (John wrote 95 AD)**

7. **Ottoman Caliphate – "ONE IS YET TO COME" (After Rome)**

8. **Revived Ottoman - "THE 8TH CONTINUES A SHORT TIME"**

LET THE PROPHET'S SPEAK

The prophet Isaiah mentions the first two empires in the master list of Satan's empires. Egypt enslaved the young nation for 400 years and attempted to drown them in the Red Sea. Assyria was the cruel empire that captured the northern 10 tribes of Israel and either killed, enslaved, or deported them into foreign lands where they never returned.

For thus says the Lord GOD: "My people went down at first into Egypt to dwell there; Then the Assyrian oppressed them without cause.

Isaiah 52:4

Daniel focuses on the five empires of Babylon, Medo-Persia, Greece, the Ottoman Caliphate, and the 8th empire of the revived Ottoman Caliphate.

In Revelation 17, we receive the completed list of all eight empires with the addition of Rome, the *"one who is."* At the time that John penned the Book of Revelation, the sixth "head" of the beast, Rome, was in power ("one is").

With the sequential order of all eight empires complete, we can now add commentary to improve our understanding.

> Here is the mind which has wisdom. The seven heads are seven mountains (Kingdoms) upon which the woman sits (the harlot religious system of Islam), and they are seven kings; five have fallen (Egypt, Assyria, Babylonian, Medo-Persia, Greece) one is (Rome), the other has not yet come (Ottoman); and when he comes (Antichrist), he must continue a short time. And the beast which was, and is not (Ottoman), is himself also an eighth (Revived Ottoman) and is one of the seven, and he goes to destruction.
>
> Revelation 17:9-11

THE HARLOT RIDES ASTRIDE THE BEAST

The context of Revelation 17 is exclusively about the two prophetic topics of the 7-headed beast (the final empire) and the false religious system (harlot/Islam) that drives the beast-empire in the last days. Our passage (verse 9) mentions something especially important about the woman that is easy to miss but significant. The text points out that the harlot "woman sits" (resides) on ALL SEVEN EMPIRES.

"Harlot" is a term that denotes a woman who prostitutes herself sexually. In Bible prophecy, the term is applied symbolically to Antichrist's system of religion that rejects true doctrine from God's Word and gives itself totally to a false system of worship.

The "woman" is the mysterious "great harlot" (Rev. 17:1) who in Revelation 17 symbolizes how the religion of Islam will be the central driving force behind the empire of Antichrist. She is portrayed as "sitting astride the beast," illustrating how Islam will be steering the reigns of the empire and be the force directing the conquests of the beast in the Tribulation.

> So he carried me away in the Spirit into the wilderness. And I saw a woman sitting on a scarlet beast which was full of names of blasphemy, having seven heads and ten horns.
>
> Revelation 17:3

This aligns with what we already know about the eighth empire being the revived Islamic Caliphate. When the apostle John says the "woman sits" on the seven empires ("sits" - where Islam resides and controls), he's saying Islam will dominate these seven regions in the last days.

> The seven heads are seven mountains (Kingdoms) upon which the woman (Islam) sits
>
> Revelation 17:9

Another name given for the harlot woman in Revelation 17 is *"Mystery Babylon, Mother of Harlots"* (Rev. 17:5). Some have suggested the harlot woman or "Mystery Babylon" represents Roman Catholicism. Is that possible? John gives us the answer.

The best way to determine the proper identification of "the woman" is simply to ask what is the religion of these seven areas today? John says "the woman sits" on all seven.

In other words, what religion today dominates the territories of Egypt, Assyria, Babylon (Iraq), Persia (Iran), Greece (Syria), Rome (Turkey) and the Ottoman Caliphate? All these areas are dominated by the antichrist religion of Islam not Catholicism.

Regarding Rome, consider the fact that Emperor Constantine moved the capitol of Rome to Byzantium, and renamed it Constantinople. What historians label as the Byzantine Empire was, in reality, the continuation of the Roman Empire in the east. And it's capitol city was what we know today as Istanbul, Turkey.

The eastern Roman empire constituted two-thirds of the duration of the Roman Empire. In terms of the sixth empire, it is clear that Rome equates to Turkey. This completes the sweep of the religion of Islam as fulfillment of John's prophecy that the "woman sits" across all seven empires.

ANTICHRIST WILL RULE FOR A "SHORT TIME"

> And they are seven kings; five have fallen, one is, the other has not yet come; and when he comes (Antichrist), he must CONTINUE FOR A SHORT TIME.
>
> Revelation 17:10

There is one more point to clarify regarding the interpretation of the phrase, *"he must continue for a short time."* Some have suggested this phrase disqualifies the seventh empire from being the Ottoman Caliphate because the Caliphate had a lengthy rule of 500 years.

Revelation 17:10 is tricky because the reading seems to point to the seventh empire, whereas, the riddle-like nature of the prophecy actually points to the eighth king. The final king of the eighth empire is Antichrist.

The "short time" designation is a reference to Antichrist's reign during the second half of the Tribulation period not the seventh empire. The reference to a short time period is made earlier in Revelation 12 with regard to the final three and a half years. Satan is cast down at the midpoint of the Tribulation and enraged because *"He knows his time is short"* (Rev. 12:12). The *"short time"* is also similar to the phrase a few chapters later in Revelation 17:12, where the kings give their authority to the beast for *"one hour."*

It is also an allusion back to the *"little moment"* of Isaiah 26, *"Come my people, enter into your rooms and close the door for a little moment until the indignation passes"* (Isa. 26:20). The concept of the *"indignation,"* so often mentioned in the prophets, points to this same period (Isaiah 30:30; 34:2; 66:14; Jer. 10:10; Dan. 11:36; Nahum 1:6; Hab. 3:12; Zeph. 3:8).

It helps to remember, the foundational passage for the time period of the last days is Daniel 9:24-27, the prophecy of "70 weeks." Since the final seven years remains unfulfilled in Daniel's prophecy (Dan. 9:27), it is widely understood that the second half of the 7-year Tribulation period, the final 3.5 years, is the *"little moment"* or *"short time"* period of God's indignations referred to by Isaiah and the prophets.

Jesus described the second half of the Tribulation as beginning with Antichrist's *"abomination of desolation"* (Matt. 24:15) and He used the phrase "great tribulation" to describe the terror of the short time leading to His return. Revelation describes it as 1260 days or 42 months that is allowed for the rule of the beast (Rev. 13:5). During his brief reign, so suddenly ended, Antichrist will exercise power unparalleled in human history.

THE RISE OF THE EIGHTH EMPIRE

We find ourselves at the threshold of identifying the eighth and final beast empire. This will be the empire of Satan's last stand at the end of this age as he seeks to wrest control of the earth from God Almighty. Satan will appoint and empower Antichrist to rule over it and trample the earth with a vengeance.

Carefully read the words of the apostle John regarding the mysterious identity of this future eighth empire.

And the beast which was, and is not, is himself also an eighth and is one of the seven, and he goes to destruction.

Revelation 17:11

The essence of what John reveals is that a beast empire that existed before – that is no longer in existence – will emerge again as an eighth empire from the previous seven. How should we interpret this verse in light of the fact that Scripture does not give us an explanation?

At the beginning of these three verses (Rev. 17:9-11), the interpreting angel who was speaking to John (Rev. 17:7) started out by saying, *"Here is the mind which has wisdom."* This is a warning to us of the challenge to understand the passage. You have to dig harder for gold! It's as if God is saying, "this is a tough passage, so don't jump to conclusions quickly, if you do, you'll probably be wrong." In the case of deciphering the eighth empire, we have to dig harder.

Some have attempted to argue that the revived beast could be any one of the previous empires such as the Assyrian Empire. But that's not the case. In reality, only the 7th empire, the Ottoman Caliphate can meet the criteria as the eighth empire.

We must remember that the story told in Revelation 17 is simply another retelling of the story told in Daniel chapters 2 and 7. When we understand that the various prophecies are all pointing us to the Islamic Caliphate, whether it be the seventh head of Revelation 17, the legs of iron in Daniel 2 or the fourth beast of Daniel 7, all of these passages are fulfilled in the Islamic Caliphate.

Some will ask why, if the Roman Empire was not included in Daniel 2 or 7, is it included in the list of empires in Revelation 17. The answer is because while Revelation 17 presents us with a comprehensive list of all of history's satanic, beast empires, Daniel 2 and 7 are not comprehensive lists detailing every one of Satan's empires.

Neither Daniel 2 or 7 include the Egyptian, the Assyrian, or the Roman Empires. As we have seen, these two chapters speak about the empires that would rise after Nebuchadnezzar in Babylon and the Roman Empire did not qualify to be included among these. It is not until we come to Revelation 12, 13 and 17 that the full list of Satanic empires is given.

As can be seen in the chart, Daniel's list includes a total of 5 empires while Revelation contains the master list of all eight empires.

COMPARISON OF DANIEL AND REVELATION

	Empire	Daniel 2	Daniel 7	Rev. 17
1	Egyptian	*not included*	*not included*	1st head
2	Assyrian	*not included*	*not included*	2nd head
3	Babylonian	Head of gold	Lion	3rd head
4	Medo-Persian	Chest and arms of silver	Bear	4th head
5	Grecian	Belly & thighs of bronze	Leopard	5th head
6	Roman	*not included*	*not included*	6th head
7	Ottoman	Legs of iron	Fourth Beast	7th head
8	Antichrist/Ottoman	Feet of iron and clay	Ten horns on the Fourth Beast	Eighth King: Healed 7th head

LIVING IN THE GAP BETWEEN THE SEVENTH AND EIGHTH BEAST EMPIRES

Why is there a gap between the seventh and eighth empires? For 4000 years Satan has empowered these seven beast empires in the Middle East to persecute the Jews and dominate Jerusalem. This all came to an end in 1922 when the last of the seven empires fell from power with the dissolution of the Ottoman Empire.

The year 2022 will mark the 100th year since the world entered the period of time referenced by John when he said, "And the beast that was… is not…" What this means for us today is that we are living in the period of the "is not." That is the gap in time between the seventh and eighth empires. But in the near future, the world will enter the time that corresponds to what John terms, "… yet is," when the seventh beast comes back to life.

As we explained, the rise and fall of the first seven empires were all consecutive and uninterrupted. Since the Ottoman Caliphate fell in 1922, why is there now a gap in time between the seventh and eighth beast empires?

In the providence of God something else of major significance took place in 1922. The Balfour Declaration was formally approved by the newly created League of Nations and ratified by treaty at the San Remo Conference. The famous document called for a national home for the Jewish people in Palestine. And was the legal impetus for the eventual rise of the modern Jewish state.

FINAL SOLUTION

However, after getting wind of the scheme to return the Jews to the promised land, Satan hatched his devious scheme and over the next decade a madman by the name of Adolph Hitler rose to power and began his ruthless, satanically-inspired "Final Solution" against the Jews. When it was over he had systematically murdered more than 6 million Jewish people.

It is impossible to fathom such horror apart from seeing the larger narrative of Satan's strategy against the Jews. From a Bible prophecy perspective, the Holocaust is best viewed as Satan's attempt to prevent the establishment of the modern State of Israel.

The devil knows that the return of Israel is a key end-time sign and that if Israel establishes their homeland it is a certain harbinger of the soon coming of Jesus to establish His Kingdom. Prophecy indicates that when the Jewish people return to the land, Jesus will soon return to the land.

But once again, through God's sovereign providence, something of wonderous importance arose from the tears and ashes of the Holocaust. In fulfillment of Biblical prophecy, the nation of Israel was miraculously reborn after her people had wandered the earth in exile for nearly 2000 years. On June 14, 1948 Israel declared her independence as a nation… and we were there!

AMERICA STANDS WITH ISRAEL

On that historic day something notable took place. Instead of a Satanic empire pouncing to devour the fledgling country, as had happened over the past millennia, this time God had the great Christian nation of the United States of America come alongside her like a big brother.

In the providence of God, America was uniquely established with an end-time purpose to support the rise and growth of Israel in the last days. In fulfilling that calling, America was the only nation to stand with Israel that day. Refusing to heed the warnings of his cabinet, Harry Truman recognized the new State of Israel when no one else would.

Then in 1967, through a miraculous series of military battles, assisted by big brother America, God's chosen people regained control over their ancient capitol, Jerusalem. In 1973 Israel narrowly missed defeat in a surprise attack by the surrounding Arab nations on Yom Kippur, Israel's most holy day. President Nixon orchestrated a massive weaponry airlift to rapidly deliver emergency aid that turned the tide for Israel.

THE GAP PERIOD ALLOWED FOR THE REBIRTH OF ISRAEL

So we can say with certainty that one of God's purposes for the 100-year gap between the seventh and eighth empires allowed for the rise of the modern State of Israel. It is no coincidence that the greatest superpower in history was there as the only friend of Israel. And that the height of American greatness perfectly parallel's the period of Israel's greatest need for support.

God is a great God and in His unfailing love and mercy He is fulfilling His promises to Israel in the last days. And now, since Israel is capable to stand on her own feet, America's role of playing big brother may be subsiding. Everything is done for God's purposes and in His perfect timing. The chosen people are about to take center stage on the world's platform.

This gap in time between the seventh and eighth empires, however, is also being utilized by Satan to prepare for his last stand against God and His chosen people. Israel's rapid rise in strength and influence has not escaped the eye of the enemy Satan who has been busy preparing for the final Holocaust. Israel finds itself closed in on all sides by Islamic nations. That's no accident!

The anti-Semitic terrorist group Hezbollah has some 100,000 missiles aimed at them on their northern border and the terrorist group Hamas is stationed on their western border in Gaza. All the while Iran is stockpiling weaponry across Iraq and Syria for the stated purpose of destroying Israel. In the program of God, Jesus Christ will emerge victorious over Satan and his minions. But at present, Satan is roaring and gearing up for the final showdown on the plains of Megiddo.

100th ANNIVERSARY OF THE TREATY OF LAUSANNE, 2023

The Turks have never forgotten the Treaty of Lausanne that stripped their empire away from them on July 24, 1923. After their defeat in WW1, the treaty caused the reduction of geography of the Turkish state forcing it to give up large territories that they had conquered. After WW1, the modern Turkish Republic was founded according to the Treaty of Lausanne that concluded with the victorious Allies in the First World War making painful conditions to the rights of the Ottoman Empire.

The Lausanne conditions support the description of the seventh beast being "mortally wounded." The Apostle John mentions the deadly wound three times (Rev. 13:3, 12, 14). He also reveals a crucial clue that it is a sword-inflicted wound which aligns precisely with the Ottoman defeat in WW1.

> And I saw one of his heads as if it had been mortally wounded, and his deadly wound was healed. And all the world marveled and followed the beast.

> And he deceives those who dwell on the earth … telling those who dwell on the earth to make an image to the beast who was wounded by the sword and lived.

> Revelation 13:4, 14

DEADLY HEAD WOUND HEALED

The wounding of the Caliphate was deep and designed to be deadly. It called for the total abolition of the Caliphate, and the exile of the Caliph and his family outside of Turkey, and the confiscation of all his assets along with the confiscation of all the land holdings of the empire across the Middle East.

The Allies were fearful the brutal regime would somehow recover and thus did everything possible to prevent the evil scourge from making a comeback. So they made a declaration that essentially banned Turkey from ever becoming an Islamic State again by constitutionally making it a secular state. The final punishment was to prevent Turkey from future oil exploration!

Fast forward 100 years later and Wala! The deadly head wound is healing! Turkey's Islamist President Erdogan thinks the 100th Anniversary of the Treaty of Lausanne should give them their land back. As the date approaches, he is growing more confident in expanding Turkey's borders and engaging in land-dispute conflicts in Syria, Iraq, Kurdistan, Cyprus, and Greece. Erdogan has announced in 2023 Turkey will enter a new era and will begin oil exploration and drilling again. The Caliphate is almost healed now with all the potential to rise very soon.

A half-dozen times in Revelation (Rev. 11:7; 13:3, 12, 14; 17:8, 11) we are told that the beast's "head wound" will heal and be revived as Satan's final empire.

It is entirely possible that very soon we will see the complete healing of the seventh empire and the rising of the eighth empire, the revived Ottoman Caliphate. Once that happens, Antichrist won't be far behind.

Chapter 6

THE ISLAMIC CONNECTION TO END-TIMES PROPHECY

A crucial aspect for understanding Bible prophecy is identifying the religion of Antichrist. While some presume that Antichrist will be a secular one world ruler, neither of these concepts about him are accurate. Instead, he is a deeply religious monarch but will never fully control the whole world (Daniel 9:26).

The missing ingredient for pulling Bible prophecy together is recognizing the deep religious nature of the empire of Antichrist. As much as he is a political ruler and head of an empire, Antichrist is also the head of a radical, end-time religious empire. Precisely described throughout the book of Revelation are key features of Islamic religious practice such as the common use of 'forced conversions' (Rev. 13:15) and beheadings (Rev. 20:4) for captured subjects that refuse to bow down. In both Daniel and Revelation the empire of Antichrist is repeatably described as being full of blasphemy.

> Then he opened his mouth in blasphemy against God, to blaspheme His name, His tabernacle, and those who dwell in heaven.   Revelation 13:6

Do you recognize the religious overtones and content in this verse? The prophetic passages about Antichrist contain religious terminology in virtually every chapter when describing his exploits in the Old and New Testaments. Nevertheless, because of the riddle-like nature of many of the prophesies, the religious character often escapes the casual reader of Scripture. It is subtle but it is always there.

Following is a chart, with phrases and activities highlighting the religious nature of Antichrist and his empire.

THE DEFIANT RELIGIOUS SYSTEM OF ANTICHRIST

- Blasphemous

  Dan.9:36; Rev.13:1,5,6; 16:9,11,21;17:3

- Worshipping

  Rev. 13:4, 8,12,15; 14:9, 11

- Spiritual Harlotry

  Rev. 17:1-3

- Wars against Christ

  Rev. 17:14; 19:19

- Wars on Jews and Christians

  Daniel 7:21,25; Rev.12:13,17; 13:7; 17:6

- Worships a god of War

  Dan. 11:38-39

- Captures Israel's Temple

  Dan. 9:27; Matt. 24:15; 2 Thess. 2:3

- Headquartered in Jerusalem

  Dan. 11:45

THE ANTICHRIST SYSTEM IS ALREADY HERE

The above descriptions and phrases are not what you would expect from a secular humanist or one-world leader. By demonstrating the spiritual and religious nature of Antichrist's kingdom, God is showing us that Antichrist will be fueled by a defiant and radical religious system with political, military, and judicial features opposing everything about God and His Word. The tenants outlined above can only be identified with the religion of Islam. What other religion on earth makes killing Jews and Christians part of their orthodoxy? And what religion today practices beheading?

Islam will become Satan's army and military force that drives the beast and Antichrist to fulfill their destructive destiny in the Tribulation. The system of Antichrist is not something the Christian world needs to be waiting for to try and figure out. It is already here, ready to march and the enemy even now has them positioned and surrounding the tiny nation of Israel!

While much of the Christian world is looking for some form of a humanistic, one-world religion to catapult Antichrist to world power, the scriptural case for an Islamic Antichrist shows that the long- awaited system of Antichrist is already here and knocking at our door, virtually unnoticed by the church.

ISLAMIC LINKAGE TO PROPHECY

The king (Antichrist) will do as he pleases. He will exalt and magnify himself above every god and will say unheard-of things against the God of gods... He will show no regard for the gods of his ancestors... Instead of them, he will honor a god of fortresses (war/Jihad); a god unknown to his ancestors… He will attack (Jihad) the mightiest fortresses with the help of a foreign god (Allah) and will honor those who acknowledge him.

Daniel 11:36-39

Although they could take up a whole book I will detail some of the prophecies and Islamic traditions that point to a coming kingdom, the eighth kingdom, that can be nothing less than the rise of the historic Islamic empire. Because of the importance of this subject in understanding the end times, my prayer is for your spiritual eyes to open as important Islamic links to prophecy are revealed.

Under the surface of many of the prophetic passages describing Antichrist is a consistent connection to the blasphemous teachings of the Quran. That connection, for instance, is what drives Antichrist to so aggressively wage Jihad on Jews and Christians during the Tribulation. In fact, most of the biblical account describing the activities and practices of Antichrist can be traced to the Quran, Shariah Law and to Islamic traditions. Most notably, Islam is the only religion on earth that adheres to them in faith and practice.

One of the direct connections to Islam in Scripture is the apostle John's teaching that the theology of Antichrist is a monotheistic, non-Christian religion precisely following the belief system of Islam (1 Jn. 2:22 – more on this in chapter 7).

Also, in light of the rise of Turkey today, it is relevant to note that Turkey, who is led by Antichrist (Gog), leads an invasion of Muslim armies against Israel in the Battle of Armageddon. The entire Gog coalition consists of Muslim nations (Ezek. 38:1-6).

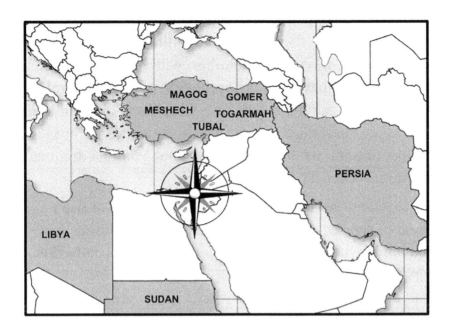

Turkey and the Invading Muslim Nations In Gog's Coalition – Ezekiel 38

It's hard not to miss that the beast empire harbors an anti-Semitic hatred of the Jewish people as well as a hatred for Christians (Dan. 7:21, 25; Rev. 13:7). The Islamic practice of capital punishment by beheading, specifically practiced by Islam, is mentioned in Revelation 20:4.

Other than Israel, Islam is the only religion who claims Jerusalem for its capitol. It makes sense then, that in prophecy, we learn Jerusalem will be captured by Antichrist and retained by the beast as its headquarters (Dan. 11:45, Matt. 24:15; 2 Thess. 2:4). The Quran commands the practice of Jihad, which is the conquering or killing of infidels. This practice is modeled by Antichrist who the Bible says is motivated by a god of war (Jihad – Dan. 9:26; 11:38-39; Revelation 6:2).

The most repeated condemnation of Antichrist and his empire is that they are filled with *blasphemy*. This is understandable if you are familiar with the Quran and its repeated claims that Jesus is not the Son of God. The religion of Islam, not Catholicism, is anti-Christ and anti-Bible and *"blasphemy"* best describes the tone and patterns of the Quran. For this reason, its blasphemy is what is most frequently condemned (Dan. 11:37; Rev. 13:5-6).

> I stood on the sand of the sea, and saw a beast rise up out of the sea, having seven heads and ten horns, and upon his horns ten crowns, and upon his heads **the** name of *blasphemy*.

> I saw a woman sitting on a scarlet beast which was full of names of *blasphemy*, having seven heads and ten horns.

> Revelation 13:1; 17:3

Other Muslim features pointing to an Islamic Empire include the Muslim-style call to prayer where its subjects bow prostrate to the ground. During the Tribulation, if they refuse to bow down, they face the Islamic practice of 'forced conversion' or death (Rev. 13:15-17).

Another vital clue in identifying the empire of Antichrist is that the geography of his empire clearly places it in the Middle East, not in Europe, China or America. Antichrist himself is referred to as 'the Assyrian' (Isaiah 10:5-6; Micah 5:5-6) which would cover portions of northern Iraq, southern Turkey and Syria. From the visions and messages of the prophets, we see one clear message - Antichrist and his coming kingdom will be centered in the Middle East.

A simple way to look at this is that if Antichrist's empire is located in the Middle East, as consistently presented in Scripture, then his religious system must be connected to Islam – there are no other choices.

Any one of these clues is significant enough to link Antichrist and his empire to Islam. The many vivid descriptions given to us in Scripture tell the frightening story that the Ottoman Caliphate will return as Satan's final beast empire and when it does, it will become the world's worst nightmare under the fanatical reign of Antichrist.

Chapter 7

THE ANTICHRIST SPIRIT OF ISLAM

And he was given a mouth speaking great things and blasphemies, and he was given authority to continue for forty-two months. Then he opened his mouth in blasphemy against God, to blaspheme His name, and to blaspheme His tabernacle, and to blaspheme those who dwell in heaven.

Revelation 13:5-6

There's evidence in Scripture to suspect Antichrist will not be anything like what many people expect. He won't be a European politician dressed in a suit and tie. He won't be dressed all in black with glowing red eyes and steam rising from his back. Nor will he stride onto the world scene with the Darth Vader theme playing in the background. All these popular concepts fail to recognize his roots!

Antichrist will be a deeply religious Muslim, possibly an Imam or Ayatollah from the Shiite sect of Islam so popular today in Iran. According to Daniel's prophecy, we first see him gaining popularity inside the revived Islamic Caliphate, *"among the ten"* (Daniel 7:8). The fact that Antichrist rises from out of one of the ten nations of the Middle East Caliphate tells us how committed to the Quran and Islamic teaching he will be. He doesn't ascend from Europe or the Vatican, nor is he a Christian or a Jew.

Apart from the one direct reference in the Bible to Antichrist, there are four other times that the apostle John uses the word in a more general sense. Each time it is in reference to a particular spirit. This spirit is defined by its denial of some specific aspects of Jesus' nature and His relationship to God the Father.

DESCRIBING THE ANTICHRIST SPIRIT

But every spirit that does not acknowledge Jesus is not from God. This is the spirit of the antichrist, which you have heard is coming and even now is already in the world. (1 John 4:3)

Who is the liar? It is the man who denies that Jesus is the Christ. Such a man is the antichrist—he denies the Father and the Son. No one who denies the Son has the Father; whoever acknowledges the Son has the Father also. (1 John 2:22–23)

Many deceivers, who do not acknowledge Jesus Christ as coming in the flesh, have gone out into the world. Any such person is the deceiver and the antichrist. (2 John 1:7)

THE THEOLOGY OF ANTICHRIST

From these verses, we learn a great deal about the theology and character of Antichrist. We see that Antichrist is an individual with a satanic spirit that is identified as a "liar" and a "deceiver" (just like Satan) whose theology specifically denies three crucial Christian doctrines as follows:

He denies…

1. That Jesus is the Christ/Messiah (Denies Jesus as the savior of the world and denies Jesus is the Messiah-Redeemer of Israel).

2. The Father and the Son (Denies the trinity and rejects any relationship of the Father to the Son). Saying he denies "the Father and the Son" is saying Antichrist rejects the doctrine of the trinity.

3. That Jesus has come in the flesh (Denies the incarnation, that Jesus is God who became man).

The religion of Islam, more than any other religion, philosophy, or belief system, fulfills the description of Antichrist's theology and his antichrist spirit. This is important to grasp because so many prophecy teachers still hold to the notion that Antichrist comes out of Rome or Europe and is therefore connected to Roman Catholicism or some form of Christianity. But as we will see in the Apostle John's breakdown of Antichrist's theology, his religious system is not from Christianity, thus making the Roman paradigm inaccurate.

Islam makes one of its highest priorities the denial of all three of the points regarding Jesus and His relationship to the Father and the trinity. In fact, we can fairly claim that Islam is a direct polemical response against those essential Christian doctrines.

ISLAM DENIES THE DEITY OF JESUS CHRIST

The religion of Islam has as one of its foundational beliefs a direct denial of Jesus as God's Son. This denial is found throughout the Quran:

In blasphemy, indeed are those that say that God is Christ, the son of Mary. (Sura 5:17; Yusuf Ali)

They say: "God hath begotten a son!"—Glory be to Him! He is self-sufficient! His are all things in the heavens and on earth! No warrant have ye for this! Say ye about Allah what ye know not? (Sura 10:68; Yusuf Ali)

They said, "The Most Gracious has begotten a son!" You have uttered a gross blasphemy. The heavens are about to shatter, the earth is about to tear asunder, and the mountains are about to crumble. Because they claim that the Most Gracious has begotten a son. It is not befitting the Most Gracious that He should beget a son. (Sura 19:88–92 Rashad Khalifa)

The Quran pronounces a curse on those who believe that Jesus is God's Son. People who say such things utter "gross blasphemies" and are likened to "unbelievers" or infidels. Without question then, in this regard, Islam is an antichrist religious system.

"Far be it from God that he should have a son!" These words encircle the inside of the Dome of the Rock in Jerusalem— the very location where for centuries God's people, the Jews, worshipped in their Temple awaiting their Messiah. This is also where Jesus, the Son of God and the Jewish Messiah, will someday rule over the earth. Islam has built a monument of utter defiance to this future reality.

ISLAM DENIES THE TRINTY

Islam applies the same claim of blasphemy to those who believe in the Trinity:

> They do blaspheme who say: Allah is one of three in a Trinity: for there is no god except One Allah. If they desist not from their word [of blasphemy], verily a grievous penalty will befall the blasphemers among them. (Sura 5:73; Yusuf Ali)

Belief in the Trinity is also defined as blasphemy. But what is the "grievous penalty" that shall befall those who believe such things? Many Muslims ironically expect their version of Jesus (Isa) to return and kill these "polytheist Trinitarian Christians."

And the Quran does not stop at denying that Jesus is the Son of God or that God exists as a Trinity.

ISLAM DENIES THE CROSS

With tears in his eyes, Paul the Apostle warned the Thessalonians that "many live as enemies of the cross of Christ" (Philippians 3:18). It should not come as a surprise then that Islam also denies the most central event of all redemptive history: the crucifixion of Jesus. Speaking of the Jews of Jesus' day, the Quran says:

> That they said [in boast], "We killed Christ Jesus the son of Mary, the Messenger of Allah"; but they killed him not, nor crucified him, but so it was made to appear to them, and those who differ therein are full of doubts, with no [certain] knowledge, but only

conjecture to follow, for of a surety they killed him not: Nay, Allah raised him up unto himself; and Allah is exalted in power, wise. (Sura 4:157–8; Yusuf Ali)

Islamic scholars put forth conflicting theories regarding exactly what happened to Jesus. Most believe he was switched at the last minute from being nailed onto the cross and replaced by someone else. After the bait and switch, Allah caught him up to heaven. Despite the inability of Muslims to arrive at any consensus regarding what happened to Jesus, they are in complete agreement on their total rejection of the gospel account, saying: He was not crucified! He never died and therefore Jesus was not the Christ who rose from the grave.

Biblically speaking, Christ's role as the risen Son of God means He is our divine Savior, the One who delivers us from our sins, and He is the coming King. In Islam, instead of delivering His followers, the Muslim Jesus (Isa) returns to earth, leads the Muslim armies against Israel and Christians, and seeks to convert or kill all the Jews and Christians on earth (Revelation 13:7).

Chapter 8

MYSTERIOUS COMING OF THE MAHDI

"If Antichrist is Islamic, it is reasonable to assume he is the Mahdi."

Jesus warned His disciples, saying, "Be careful that no one leads you astray! For many will come in My name, saying, 'I am the Messiah,' and will lead many astray" (Matthew 24:4–5).

From a Christian perspective, before the true Messiah, the Lord Jesus Christ, returns in the clouds of heaven, there will be counterfeit messiahs (antichrists) who will deceive many.

In the Islamic world, the belief and expectation in the coming of the Mahdi, Islam's messianic figure, is preparing the way for Antichrist. Twenty-five percent of the world's population is Muslim today, and the vast majority are waiting for their messiah, the Mahdi, to return. Most amazingly, the coming of the Muslim Mahdi parallels the Biblical account of Antichrist.

This parallelism is more than just a coincidence. The entire story of the Mahdi is purposely crafted by the enemy to pattern the Biblical account of Antichrist, Satan's great deceiver in the last days. To describe this phenomenon, I like to use the term anti-parallelism. It suggests that the parallels have OPPOSITE PURPOSES. The Quran is full of anti-parallelism in correlation to the Bible, and the coming of the Mahdi is the pinnacle of this demonic methodology.

PARALLELS OF ANTICHRIST AND THE MAHDI

The religion of Islam has an end-time belief system that mysteriously parallels Bible prophecy. Pious Muslim's are required to believe in and adhere to the Islamic end-time expectations known as the Final Day. I find that interesting! Muslim's are required to accept Islamic teaching on the 'Final Day.' Why do you suppose the Islamic version of last-day events is so important? Satan needs the Muslim world prepared and ready to anticipate them to come to pass. It's as if the devious enemy has designed a 'special-forces' religious system to combat the Biblical account of last-day events as his primary weapon for destroying Israel and defeating Christ at His Second Coming. There are just too many parallels for it to be a coincidence. The most anticipated and central sign Muslims wait for in the last days is the coming of a man known as "the Mahdi." In Arabic, it means "the Guided One."

Just who is this "awaited one" that the Islamic world longs for, and what will he do that has Muslims in such a state of anticipation?

In the simplest of terms, the Mahdi is Islam's messiah or savior.

It is fair to say that the "rising" of the Mahdi is to the majority of Muslims what the return of Jesus is to Christians. While Christians await the return of Jesus the Messiah to fulfill all of God's prophetic promises to the people of God, Muslims await the appearance of the Mahdi to fulfill Satan's purposes.

Throughout the Islamic world today, there is a call for the restoration of the Islamic caliphate. The position of "Caliph" in Islam is the official office of the ruler of Islam. Muslims view the Caliph as the vice regent for Allah on the earth. It is important to understand that when Muslims call for the restoration of the Caliphate, it is ultimately the Mahdi that they call for. The Mahdi is the awaited final ruler of Islam, and Muslims everywhere will be obligated to follow him.

THE TIMING OF MAHDI'S RETURN

There are many similarities of the Biblical Antichrist and Islam's messiah figure, the Mahdi. According to Islamic teaching, the Mahdi's ascendancy to power takes place at the time of a final peace agreement between the Arabs and Israel. Interestingly, the peace agreement will be made for a period of seven years, and the period of this seven-year peace agreement will likewise be the period of the reign of the Mahdi, the Islamic messiah. Sound familiar?

The Mahdi is said to have been born in 879 A.D. and is believed by Shia Muslims to still be alive but hidden from mankind in 'occultation' until a time of such upheaval on the earth that only his reappearance will rescue mankind. The purpose of his coming is to bring an age of global peace. This so called "peace" is "Islamic peace," the age when all mankind is living in submission to Allah and under Shariah Law.

THE MAHDI SPIRIT OF IRAN

The founders and leaders of Iran are fanatical in their expectation of the coming Mahdi in the last days. It is also the basis of Tehran's foreign and military policies. Because of this, it is impossible to overemphasize the Iran regime's visceral commitment to it.

The Imam Mahdi is invoked in every public gathering, both civil and military, and they readily admit he is the singular inspiration for every policy, every tactic, every mission. Accordingly, in Iran, the Mahdi is nothing less than the regime's reason for its existence and, as such, its singular motivation for the future.

In the words of Iran's Supreme leader Ayatollah Khamenei, "The Iranian nation enjoys a great privilege today: the atmosphere of the country is an atmosphere of Imam Mahdi." Khamenei states, "many of our great scholars have personally met with this beloved [Imam] during his occultation; many have made a pledge to him in person."

Muslims around the world are waiting for the Mahdi. Of the numerous things that this "Twelfth Imam" is said to accomplish, most notable is that he will be able to interpret the dark passages of the Quran, settle the disputes between the sects and vindicate Shiite doctrine.

THE MAHDI GOES TO JERUSALEM

Believers who search the Word and study Bible prophecy should find it significant that the Mahdi wants to rule from Jerusalem. One of the great themes of end-time prophecy is the battle over Jerusalem. Satan will use the Mahdi to lay claim to God's city and move him (Antichrist) to capture the eastern half of Jerusalem in the middle of the Tribulation (Zech. 14:1-3; Matt. 24:15-16).

In their book *Al Mahdi and the End Time*, authors Muhammad ibn Izzat and Muhammad Arif write:

"Jerusalem will be the location of the rightly guided caliphate and the center of Islamic rule, which will be headed by Imam al-Mahdi... This will abolish the leadership of the Jews."

How interesting that Muslims believe the Mahdi will rule from Jerusalem. Followers of Islam are being deceived by Satan to such an extent they will accept everything Antichrist does to be the activities of their messiah! The followers of Allah may feel the Mahdi is their messiah, but we know him as Antichrist.

He (Antichrist) will pitch his royal tents (make his capitol) between the seas at the beautiful holy mountain (Temple Mount). Yet he will come to his end, and no one will help him.

Daniel 11:45

Satan is the great deceiver who has deceived Muslims to be looking for and anticipating the soon return of their messiah, the Mahdi. He has accomplished his deception through the teachings of the Quran and through Islamic traditions that are not part of the Quran, which he can change and adapt as the situation arises.

The powerful deceptions of Satan now have one-quarter of the world today eagerly awaiting the arrival of Antichrist with open arms. When the Rapture occurs, and Antichrist begins to rise, the Islamic world will be ecstatic to accept the Mahdi, the Twelfth Imam, as the coming of their long-awaited messiah.

From a Biblical perspective, the coming of their messiah marks the arrival of Antichrist.

Chapter 9

THE RISE OF ANTICHRIST BEGINS:

HIJACKING THE CALIPHATE

The ten horns are ten kings… After them, another king will arise (Antichrist), he will subdue three kings.

Daniel 7:24

According to the prophet Daniel, the first sign of Antichrist on earth is when he begins to rise through the ranks of the revived Ottoman Caliphate. His rise sparks a bloody civil war that supernaturally opens the door for him to step up and to take control of the empire.

Satan is the great deceiver and often takes Biblical truth and distorts it in the Quran and Islamic teaching to fit his devious narrative. We see this idea in how Antichrist imitates the pattern of Jesus rising to prominence as Israel's Messiah.

ANTICHRIST MIMICS THE LIFE OF JESUS

To mirror God's path for Jesus, Antichrist will begin to gather loyal followers who perceive him as Islam's messiah figure, just as Jesus was perceived as Israel's Messiah. He will portray himself as the long-awaited Shiite messiah, the "Mahdi," claiming he's the Twelfth Imam, the final descendent in the bloodline of Muhammad, even as Jesus was prophesied to be a descendant of the bloodline of David (Revelation 22:16). Just as God sent forth Jesus His Son, "in the fulness of time" (Galatians 4:1), Satan will bring forth Islam's messiah, the "lawless one," in his time.

> The coming of the lawless one is according to the working of Satan, with all power, signs, and lying wonders.
>
> 2 Thessalonians 2:9

In the early days of the revived Islamic Caliphate, it is likely that Antichrist will first appear by gathering a following through his insightful teaching, just as Jesus did. He will gain popularity by his insights and memory of the Quran and follow a strict adherence to Shariah Law, just as Jesus honored and obeyed the Mosaic law (Matt. 5:17). Unlike the humility of Jesus, Antichrist has a boasting tongue, and blasphemous speech pointed out as outstanding features.

> He was given a mouth speaking great things (proud words) and blasphemies.
>
> Revelation 13:5

> He had a mouth speaking pompous words.
>
> Daniel 7:8, 20

Scripture points out that his boasting is unique because it is directed against the "Most High." He might say things like, "this is the hour of the (Muslim) 'last day' when the true god Allah will subdue the earth and rid the world of the scourge of Christianity and the Jewish people."

He shall speak pompous words against the Most High,
and shall persecute the saints of the Most High.

Daniel 7:25

With the power of Satan promoting him (2 Thess. 2:9), Antichrist's popularity will soar and begin overflowing into the streets. Picture the mass demonstrations that took place across the Middle East during the Arab Spring uprisings (2011-12). If the Islamic world gets wind that their Mahdi has finally arrived, the fervor of anticipation and support will be far more explosive than the Arab Spring. When word gets out he's already part of the Caliphate and efforts are underway to support him as Caliph, the movement won't be stopped. The end-time arrival of the Mahdi to rule the Caliphate is the hope of the Muslim world!

Consider that Antichrist's rise possibly begins in his home country of Syria, Iraq, or Iran, and his popularity will quickly spread to the other countries of the Caliphate. Before the leadership of the Caliphate realize what's happening, a flood of endless demonstrations and chanting will erupt across the ten nation empire calling for the leadership to recognize the Mahdi as Muhammad's rightful heir of the Caliphate and to move aside.

SUNNI VERSUS SHIITE

The source of the Mahdi's popularity energizing his movement is an ancient battle inside of Islam over who has the right to rule the Islamic Empire. Islam split over this subject after the death of Muhammad, with the Sunni faction believing that any pious Muslim can be chosen to rule the Caliphate, and the Shiite sect believing only a Muslim in the bloodline of Muhammad has the right to rule the empire.

This seems to align with Daniel's description of the empire in chapter two, where he refers to the ten kings being divided and unable to mix together. Daniel portrays the empire as lacking unity and possessing deep differences. This would be an apt description if some of the ten kings belonged to the sect of Sunni Islam and the others belonged to the sect of Shiite Islam.

> Just as you saw that the feet and toes were partly of baked clay and partly of iron, so this will be a divided kingdom; yet it will have some of the strength of iron in it, even as you saw iron mixed with clay. As the toes were partly iron and partly clay, so this kingdom will be partly strong and partly brittle. And just as you saw the iron mixed with baked clay, so the people will be a mixture and will not remain united, any more than iron mixes with clay.

> Daniel 2:41-43

BLOODY CIVIL WAR TO CONTROL THE CALIPHATE

With Turkey being the head of the Caliphate, it's reasonable to expect that the first caliph of the empire will also be a follower of Sunni Islam. It will appear, therefore, that Sunni teaching dominates the theology and practices in the establishment of the ten-king Caliphate. But the Mahdi is Shiite and has other ideas.

There is reason to believe the wave of support from his enthusiastic followers will rapidly deepen the Sunni-Shiite divide among the ten leaders of the Caliphate. This will create somewhat of a split in the new empire, with the Iranian-led

Shiite members throwing their military support behind the meteoric rise of the Mahdi (Antichrist).

THREE OF THE TEN KINGS TAKEN OUT

At this point, Daniel simply says that Antichrist "will subdue three kings" (Daniel 7:24) and "three of the first horns were plucked out by their roots" (Daniel 7:8) and "three fell" (Daniel 7:20).

Daniel provides minimal details about this bloody civil war over control of the empire. This seems to highlight the fearless speed and success with which Antichrist moves to settle the issue. As a result of his immense popularity among the Shiite kings, he'll be given the support of their military apparatus, and in an unexpected blitz, he will simultaneously take out three of the ten original kings.

In an instant, three of the 10 kings are eviscerated! GONE! With the possibility of Iranian nuclear arms at his disposal using un-manned drones or precision-guided missiles, it is not difficult to see how this could be accomplished. In 2020, something similar occurred when President Donald Trump took out Qassem Soleimani in his car while driving away from the Iraqi airport. Antichrist will not only achieve his goal with the help of laser-guided technology, but he will also have the added guiding hand of Satan himself.

Antichrist is not attempting here to destroy the Caliphate. He simply plans to eliminate the three opposition kings in such a precision-like manner the other seven kings get the message and capitulate without a fight. It's likely, the three opposing kings are Sunni leaders demanding a Sunni Muslim, not a Shiite Muslim like Antichrist, remain ruler of the Caliphate.

MISSION ACCOMPLISHED: OPPOSITION REMOVED

The opposing Sunni leaders have seen enough of how their new Shiite leader operates and will not make the mistake of voicing further opposition. He has made his statement loud enough to prevent future opposition. Antichrist emerges from the first and only civil war for control of the Caliphate with absolute rule. There will be no future challenges to his authority from inside the empire.

There is one more thing to clear up about Antichrist's defeat of three of the original ten kings. Since Antichrist "uproots three of the kings," yet Scripture also talks about all ten kings still living later on in both Daniel and Revelation, we can assume Antichrist installs three new kings who are more loyal to him to govern the countries of the three defeated kings.

The prophet Daniel makes it clear that ten kings, not seven, are still ruling together at the end of the Tribulation. This is illustrated by the ten toes on Nebuchadnezzar's image being smashed by the "rock of Christ" when He returns at His Second Coming (Daniel 2:42-45). All ten kings are alive and finally overthrown when Jesus returns to establish His Millennial Kingdom.

> In the time of those (ten) kings, the God of heaven will set up a kingdom that will never be destroyed, nor will it be left to another people. It will crush all those kingdoms and bring them to an end, but it will itself endure forever. This is the meaning of the vision of the rock cut out of a mountain, but not by human hands—a rock that

broke the iron, the bronze, the clay, the silver and the gold to pieces.

Daniel 2:44-45

Chapter 10

THE PEACE DEAL TRIGGERS THE 7-YEAR TRIBULATION

He (Antichrist) will confirm a covenant with many (Israel and the other parties) for one seven (seven years). In the middle of the 'seven' he will put an end to sacrifice and offering. And at the temple he will set up an abomination that causes desolation, until the end that is decreed is poured out on him.

Daniel 9:27

Successfully negotiating a Middle East peace deal has been elusive for the last fifty years. But in God's timing, it will surely come to pass and fulfill a major end-time sign. As soon as Antichrist has consolidated his control over the Caliphate, he will turn his attention to a peace treaty with Israel. The negotiation period up to signing the agreement is the final phase before the start of the Tribulation. The period in the run-up to signing the treaty is also the last time frame for the Rapture to occur if it has not already happened. The Apostle Paul makes it clear that the church is raptured before the identity of Antichrist is revealed.

Don't you remember that when I was with you I used to tell you these things? And now you know what is holding him (Antichrist) back, so that he may be revealed at the proper time. For the secret power of lawlessness is already at work; but the one who now holds it back (Holy Spirit) will continue to do so till he is taken out of the way (Rapture). And then the lawless one will be revealed, whom the Lord Jesus will overthrow with the breath of his mouth and destroy by the splendor of his coming.

2 Thessalonians 2:5-8

Not only does the rise of Antichrist play a role in the timing of the Rapture of the church, but it is also significant for the timing of the Tribulation period. In Daniel 9:27, the prophet Daniel indicates that when Antichrist makes a seven-year covenant with Israel, it marks the beginning of the Tribulation. In addition, we are told that halfway through the seven-year peace term (three and a half years), Antichrist will break the covenant and turn against Israel.

Daniel describes that Antichrist will "confirm" a covenant. This could be a confirmation of a new treaty he has personally drafted and helped negotiate, or more likely; it indicates he confirms a plan that has already been put forth.

PEACE IS ILLUSIVE

There have been numerous plans put forth by the United States and the United Nations trying to resolve the Israeli and Palestinian issue. Almost every US President since Jimmy Carter has added and adopted various proposals between Israel and the Palestinians.

The various plans put forth prior to the Trump Plan were rejected for many reasons, but from Israel's perspective, they were rejected because they were written from an anti-Israel, pro-Palestinian perspective. More importantly, they failed because it wasn't God's timing.

The most exhaustive plan to date is the Trump plan released in a two-phase roll-out in 2019 and 2020. The details of the Trump plan are so thorough they have probably laid much of the groundwork for the future plan between Antichrist and Israel.

Daniel 9:27 also says that Antichrist *"will confirm a covenant with many."* Exactly who the *"many"* is referring to is not stated, but the suggestion is that multiple parties will become part of the agreement.

We know that Israel is among the *"many"* because the context of Daniel 9:27 relates to the Jewish people and Jerusalem. The other parties central to the treaty would be the Palestinians as well as the Ottoman Caliphate, which is now ruled by Antichrist, who Daniel says will *"confirm the covenant."* Jordan would need to be part of the treaty since they border Israel on the east bank of the Jordan River and also because they play such a key role managing the Temple Mount.

It's also reasonable to assume the countries of Syria, which borders Israel to the north, and Egypt, which borders her to the south, will be signatories. Other possibilities could include the Arab States who have formed a coalition with Israel through the Abraham Accords. Israel's Arab partners could play a significant negotiating role in the vital stumbling point of Israel building the Temple on the Temple Mount. This issue has always been a sticking point for previous plans.

DIVIDING ISREAL: MISTAKE OF THE TWO-STATE PLAN

One element that seems certain is that the final peace proposal, at its core, will be designed around the framework of a Two-State Plan that calls for dividing Israel. When Israel accepts these terms and officially becomes signatory to an agreement that surrenders parts of the Holy Land, God's wrath immediately falls and will not let off for seven years. By forcing Israel to relinquish land, the world will face swift punishment.

God never intended to miraculously bring Israel back into their ancient homeland just so Israel could surrender some of the land for an Islamic State, let alone one who publicly hates Israel and who worships the false god Allah who stands against the Lord!

Not only will God not allow an Islamic State to share the promised land with Israel, but according to the prophet Joel, dividing the land crosses God's red line and becomes the reason for God's punishment of the nations in the battle of Armageddon,

> In those days and at that time, when I restore the fortunes of Judah and Jerusalem, I will gather all nations and bring them down to the Valley of Jehoshaphat. There I will put them on trial for what they did to my inheritance, my people Israel, because they scattered my people among the nations and divided up My land.

Joel 3:1-2

Notice the last two words in the above verse that say, "My land." God reminds us that the promised land is not Israel's to give up and that it belongs to Him. God gave the land to Israel permanently, and He is not planning to surrender it to anyone else.

THE SO-CALLED "WEST-BANK" BELONGS TO ISRAEL

There are hundreds of passages concerning God's heart for Israel in the Bible that discuss His promises to restore the Jewish people physically to their land and then to restore them spiritually to Him.

Scripture records one-hundred and seventy references that the Holy Land belongs to Israel. So there's no confusion, fifteen times, God describes the boundaries and borders of Israel's land. Twelve times the land is described as an "eternal possession" that God gave to Abraham, Isaac, Jacob, and their descendants.

From God's perspective, the Holy Land still belongs to the Jewish people today. Some fifty-five times, the Bible reminds us that God confirmed the land to Abraham and his descendants by an everlasting oath. The story of God's original oath to Abraham appears in Genesis chapter fifteen. And sixty-four times, God declares His intention to bring His people back to their original homeland in the last days from the nations where they were scattered. Israel's homeland includes all the land Israel gained in the miraculous Six-Day War in 1967, including the Sinai Peninsula, the Gaza Strip, all the West Bank, and the Golan Heights.

In Ezekiel's presentation of the battle of Gog and Magog, we find another verse saying that God lays claim to the "mountains" of Israel calling them, "My mountains." The mountains that God is referring to include the mountainous region of Judea, Samaria and Jerusalem. God points out that the West Bank mountains of Judea and Samaria do not belong to the Palestinians but instead belong to Him, and by extension, Israel and no one else.

> I will call for a sword against Gog throughout all My mountains, says the Lord GOD. Every man's sword will be against his brother.
>
> Ezekiel 38:21

Dividing the land of Israel involves changing the borders that God established long ago. To emphasize the permanence of the borders, God repeats the details throughout Scripture. Man does not have the authority to change God's pre-determined, eternal border lines. If anyone is foolish enough to attempt to change Israel's boundaries, He gives a stern warning that He'll make the boundary stones so heavy that whoever tries to move them will get hurt,

> On that day, when all the nations of the earth are gathered against her, I will make Jerusalem an immovable rock for all the nations. All who try to move it will injure themselves.
>
> Zechariah 12:3

TOUCHING DOWN ON THE MOUNT OF OLIVES

Questions regarding Israel's land rights is one of the central issues driving end-time prophecy and the international debate that is raging today. The question to answer is... does the West Bank real estate belong to the modern State of Israel in the same way it belonged to ancient Israel when God first laid out Israel's borders?

The answer is in a clue we find regarding the location of Christ's Second Coming. We find it in Zechariah's prophecy. At the end of the seven-year Tribulation, when the armies of Antichrist are about to defeat Israel, Jesus returns in the clouds to rescue them by planting His feet down on the Mount of Olives. Bullseye!

> And in that day His feet will stand on the Mount of Olives which faces Jerusalem on the east. And the Mount of Olives shall be split in two, from east to west, making a very large valley; half of the mountain shall move toward the north and half of it toward the south.
>
> Zechariah 14:4

Christ's landing creates an end-time version of the parting of the Red Sea by dramatically dividing the Mount of Olives in half! As His feet touch down, the mountain parts, in the same way, God parted the waters of the Red Sea. A supernatural escape route is formed, allowing the Israelites to flee from Antichrist through a new valley just as they did when they passed through the walled waters of the Red Sea.

While the UN, EU, and most world governments today claim the Mount of Olives is part of the so-called West Bank and belongs to the Palestinians, the strategic location of Christ's landing on top of the Mount of Olives says otherwise.

We can be assured that, from God's perspective, the West Bank is still the "promised land," giving Israel a valid claim to all the land God originally granted them. With pinpoint accuracy, the Second Coming settles this hotly debated topic! It speaks louder than the United Nations, the Palestinian

Authority, or the Arab League and leaves no doubt the West Bank belongs to the modern State of Israel.

> Then you shall flee through My mountain valley, for the mountain valley shall reach to Azal.

> Zechariah 14:5

Notice that once again, the Lord uses the personal pronoun "My mountain valley " in describing this newly created valley in the center of the Mt. of Olives. The world claims it belongs to the Palestinians and that Israel has no right to "steal it" from them. The world may call it the West Bank, but God calls it "My valley."

This confirms that the land promises given to Israel in the Abrahamic covenant were unconditional and eternal and that supporting Israel's right to the land is also supporting God's Word.

WHY SEVEN YEARS?

There remains seven years still unfulfilled in Daniel's 70-Week prophecy of Daniel 9:24-27. In the details provided, we are told that the covenant between Israel and Antichrist will also be for 7 years, thus fulfilling the time limit of the prophecy.

There are two good reasons for the seven-year term limit of the future peace plan signed by Antichrist and Israel. One deals with prophecy, and another one is possibly for the more legal and practical issues to be worked out between the two states.

As for the prophetic reason, the seven-year Tribulation fulfills that missing seven-year period in Daniel's prophecy.

The prophecy of Daniel's Seventy Weeks lays out God's calendar for Israel. In the prophecy, Daniel explained that Israel and their holy city Jerusalem would be allotted seventy weeks of years or 490 years for God to accomplish all His plans with them before the establishment of His Messianic Kingdom. This complex and accurate prophecy lays out all that God has planned for Israel, with sixty-nine of those weeks (483 years) historically accounted for.

However, the Seventieth Week (seven years - Daniel 9:27) is reserved for future fulfillment in the last days before Jesus' Second Coming.

The interruption between the sixty-ninth and seventieth week includes the 2000-year Church Age, which ends with the Rapture. At some point after the Rapture, Antichrist will appear and negotiate the covenant with Israel. It's not the Rapture that starts the Tribulation. Rather it's when Antichrist confirms the covenant with Israel that triggers the seven-year clock.

The practical reason for the seven-year timeline is likely for Israel to fully transition out of Judea and Samaria, the so-called West Bank. The seven-year period would serve as an appropriate length for Israel and the Palestinians to resolve the many issues surrounding the establishment of two states. Major issues like housing, utilities, infrastructure, checkpoints and government facilities will all need to be worked out and then built during the seven-year transition. It is a large undertaking to create an entirely new country inside of an existing country, and it will not be accomplished overnight. It will also require both governments to draft large slates of laws for the two states to function side by side, with both sides approving the slate of new laws.

Chapter 11

SATAN TAKES THE SANCTUARY

According to prophecy, Israel will build its temple near the beginning of the seven-year Tribulation period. At that time, Israel's next temple, often described as their third temple or Tribulation temple, will be built where it once stood on the 35-acre Temple Mount in Jerusalem.

The first Temple was built by Solomon and destroyed in 586 BC by the Babylonians. The second Temple was built by Zerubbabel after Israel returned from exile and was then significantly enlarged in the time of Christ by Herod the Great. It was completely destroyed by the Romans in 70 AD, and Israel has been without a temple for almost 2000 years.

There are numerous passages showing that the Jewish people will have a temple in the end times.

> When you see the abomination of desolation, spoken of by Daniel the prophet, standing in the holy place (Israel's temple on the Temple Mount ["holy place"] being taken over by Antichrist)
>
> Matthew 24:15

He (Antichrist) opposes and exalts himself above all that is called God or that is worshiped, so that he sits as God in the temple of God, showing himself that he is God.

2 Thessalonians 2:3-4

DOME OF THE ROCK ON THE TEMPLE MOUNT

Today there is a problem with Israel building the temple. In an obvious maneuver showing how Satan uses the religion of Islam for his purposes, Satan has captured the Temple Mount. On the Temple Mount, today sits two Muslim "holy sites" known as the Dome of the Rock and the al-Aqsa Mosque. This satanic takeover has prevented Israel from building their temple ever since Israel captured the Temple Mount in the 1967 Six-Day War.

At some point in the future negotiations for peace between Israel and Antichrist, the solution to this conundrum will be resolved through a unique sharing arrangement described in Revelation chapter 11.

Then I was given a reed like a measuring rod. And the angel stood, saying, Rise and measure the temple of God, the altar, and those who worship there. But leave out the court which is outside the temple, and do not measure it, for it has been given to the Gentiles. And they will tread the holy city underfoot for forty-two months.

Revelation 11:1-2

SHARING THE TEMPLE MOUNT

The State of Israel and the Caliphate leaders of the Islamic Empire will come to terms by agreeing to a shared relationship of the Temple Mount. In this arrangement, both the Islamic holy sites and Israel's temple will co-exist together on the Temple Mount.

Notice in this prophecy about Israel's future temple that the Apostle John is told to go ahead and measure the future temple. It seems a bit unusual for John to be handed a measuring rod and told to go start laying out the dimensions of the temple. What's the purpose of this scene? There are two essential reasons why God wants John to begin measuring the temple.

The first reason is because God wants us to know for certain that Israel will have a real temple with real measurements once again during the Tribulation period. What this means is that the Lord is making the church aware that Israel will build their temple near the start of the Tribulation. As a result, preparations for building the temple can now serve as a key end-time sign in understanding how close we are getting to the Tribulation period. The closer we get, the more prominent the temple debate will become in Israel's Knesset and the peace negotiations.

DON'T CONSTRUCT THE OUTER COURTS

Secondly, John's measuring of the temple illustrates another end-time sign about the temple we should be aware of. Did you notice that the angel cautioned him to stop measuring the area of the outside courts?

But leave out the court which is outside the temple, and do not measure it, for it has been given to the Gentiles.

Revelation 11:2

The outer courts were large areas set up for the temple activity and where the Jewish people gathered. The reason given why John should not measure the courtyard area is because there isn't enough room on the Temple Mount. This insightful prophecy has already come to pass since the devious construction of the Dome of the Rock over the site of Israel's former temple.

The angel states that the courtyard areas are controlled by Gentiles which we know in this case refers to the Muslims and their Islamic holy sites. That's why there isn't enough room. The prophecy describes that this issue will ultimately be resolved by a unique sharing arrangement on the Temple Mount between Israel and Islam.

Israel will build their temple without the historic outer courtyard because that space will remain under the control of Muslims. According to this prophecy, the Muslim Dome of the Rock is not going anywhere, but it will be joined alongside Israel's temple.

Today there is no temple. That's why, three times a day, many Jews pray at the Western Wall in Jerusalem, crying out, "May our temple be rebuilt in this day here in the holy city."

The Tribulation Temple will likely not be built until the start of the Tribulation when permission is given to fully access the Temple Mount as part of the terms of the treaty between Antichrist and Israel (Daniel 9:27).

CALLS FOR THE TEMPLE GETTING LOUDER

Orthodox Jews in Israel today are beginning to call for greater Jewish access to the Temple Mount and even for the construction of the Temple. In 2019, for the first time in the history of the modern state of Israel, several Orthodox Jewish political parties ran for the Knesset with their political plank stating it was time for Israel to build the temple. In the meantime, everything for the new temple is already prepared and ready.

The Temple Institute in Jerusalem has spent an estimated $30 million on preparations for the temple. When touring Israel or viewing online, you can visit their impressive collection of everything from the gold-plated ark of the covenant to the robes for the priesthood and even the temple cornerstone.

Nothing will bolster Antichrist as a man of diplomatic skills more than allowing for the rebuilding of Israel's temple on the Temple Mount. Many scholars believe that the ancient Jewish temple was behind the Eastern Gate on the eastern side of the Temple Mount wall. The Eastern Gate is now sealed. There seems to be plenty of room behind the Eastern Gate to rebuild the Jewish temple without harming the Dome of the Rock. Both the Jewish Temple and the Dome of the Rock would be side by side, aligning with the prophecy of Revelation 11:2.

What would be a greater testimony to the peace and unity espoused by Antichrist than these two great religions so long at odds now sharing the sacred site? It is possible that when Israel negotiates the terms for the two-state plan that they will demand the temple be built on the Temple Mount in exchange. Apparently, both Antichrist and Israel will see the arrangement as a win-win situation. The Palestinians receive the West Bank for their new Palestinian State and Israel sees the temple as the long-awaited answer to their prayers.

It makes sense that if Antichrist pulls off this astounding achievement, then he will want to come and celebrate the diplomatic success. Maybe it will be an official ceremony with leaders from the UN along with all the nations signing the historic Middle East peace plan. Every news outlet in every nation will be covering the events with Muslim imams and Jewish rabbis gathered together on the Temple Mount in mutual respect. All the world will feel that there is, at last, peace in the Middle East.

Now let's fast forward three and a half years later.

ANTICHRIST BREAKS THE COVENANT

As prophesied by Daniel, the peace between Antichrist and Israel will be broken after three and a half years.

> In the middle of the 'seven' he will put an end to sacrifice and offering. And at the temple he will set up an abomination that causes desolation, until the end that is decreed is poured out on him.

> Daniel 9:27

Three and a half years after the historic signing of the peace deal, Antichrist will do an about-face and break his covenant with Israel.

The question needs to be asked, "What brings Antichrist's sudden about-face from guaranteeing peace to slaughtering innocent Jewish citizens?"

The book of Revelation has a lot to say about the activities of Satan during the Tribulation period, with chapter twelve dedicated for that purpose. The chapter informs us that Satan knows his time is short! Satan recognizes from Daniel's prophecy that once the covenant is signed, Jesus Christ will return in seven years to establish His Millennial Kingdom, and if that happens, Satan will be chained and incarcerated for one-thousand years, a fate he's desperate to prevent (Revelation 20:1-3).

There is another decisive event that sets the stage for the dramatic events of the middle of the Tribulation. In God's sovereign plan, Satan is suddenly and irrevocably evicted from the heavenlies in the middle of the Tribulation period. The event is recorded in Revelation chapter 12 where heaven erupts into a war between Michael and his angels against Satan and his angels over Satan's presence in the heavenlies.

Satan and his demonic hordes who have assembled an empire of darkness in the spiritual realms of the second heaven are soundly defeated.

Driven out of the heavenlies is a game-changer for the prince of darkness who finds himself barred from heaven. Defeated and now remanded to earth, Satan is furious knowing that his time is short,

> So the great dragon was cast out, that serpent of old, called the Devil and Satan, who deceives the whole world; he was cast to the earth, and his angels were cast out with him. Therefore rejoice, O heavens, and you who dwell in them! Woe to the inhabitants of the earth and the sea! For the devil has come down to you, having great wrath, because he knows that he has a short time.
>
> Revelation 12:9, 12

REMNANT FLEES TO THE MOUNTAINS

With the anger of Satan roused, it sets off the dynamic events in the middle of the seven-year Tribulation. Realizing he can no longer wait seven years for the terms of the covenant to play out and for Israel to vacate the West Bank, Satan sets his sights on Jerusalem and incites Antichrist to begin his military campaign south into the Holy Land.

> And he (Antichrist) shall plant the tents of his palace between the seas and the glorious holy mountain (Jerusalem); yet he shall come to his end, and no one will help him.
>
> Daniel 11:45

Jesus gave special instructions to the Jewish people living in the so-called West Bank at this time, telling them to *"flee to the mountains"* to escape Antichrist's persecution,

> Then let those who are in Judea (West Bank) flee to the mountains. Let him who is on the housetop not go down to take anything out of his house. And let him who is in the field not go back to get his clothes. But woe to those who are pregnant and to those who are nursing babies in those days! And pray that your flight may not be in winter or on the Sabbath. For then there will be great tribulation, such as has not been since the beginning of the world until this time, no, nor ever shall be.
>
> Matthew 24:16-21

The West Bank families who survive Antichrist's assault by following Jesus' instructions to *"flee to the mountains,"* may be directed by the Lord into the mountainous region of

Petra southeast of the Dead Sea, into the country of Jordan. The prophet Daniel says that Jordan will not fall under Antichrist's control and could therefore be preserved by God as a safe haven for these Jewish families (Dan. 11:41).

When the entourage of evicted Jews arrive safely in Petra, they become the special Jewish remnant protected and fed by the Lord during the second half of the Tribulation. God miraculously takes care of them and meets their every need for three and a half years, just as He took care of the children of Israel in their wilderness wanderings for forty years.

> Then the woman fled into the wilderness, where she has a place prepared by God, that they should feed her there one thousand two hundred and sixty days.
>
> Revelation 12:6

CONVERTING THE TEMPLE TO A MOSQUE

As the Caliphate armies take control of the West Bank and East Jerusalem, Antichrist will establish the Temple Mount as his headquarters and the operational center for the government of the Islamic empire. What a sight that will be!

Satan's man will now sit on the place of God's throne! Where once stood ancient Israel's glorious temple with the presence of God in the Holy of Holies, now sits Antichrist, filled like Judas Iscariot, with the very spirit of Satan.

The sacred 35 acres of the Temple Mount, including the Al-Aqsa Mosque, the Dome of the Rock, and Israel's new temple, will now showcase the activities of Antichrist for three and a half years, right up until Christ's Second Coming. Once Israel's temple falls into his hands, Antichrist will commit the "abomination of desolation" prophesied by both Daniel and

Jesus (Daniel 9:27; 11:31; 12:11; Matthew 24:15). Although the specifics are not provided, the simple definition for the abomination is that the temple is made unclean and therefore unfit for Jewish worship.

What might occur at this point is the conversion of Israel's temple into a mosque with tall minarets and with the extra-large loud speakers used for the Muslim call to prayer. One can only imagine the thrill of the Islamic hordes now crowding the streets of Jerusalem at the blast coming off Israel's former temple. Five times a day, the deafening call to prayer repeats the single most blasphemous religious phrase on earth, *"there is no god but Allah."*

Converting captured religious facilities into Islamic use and for mosques was a common practice of the Ottomans, more recently practiced by ISIS. The conversion of Israel's temple into a mosque would surely qualify as an abomination that desecrates Israel's temple.

During the 500 year reign of the Ottoman Caliphate, whenever they conquered new lands, the practice was either to tear down the churches or convert them to mosques. If the churches were suitable, they would take down the crosses and replace them with the Muslim quarter-moon insignia, then build minarets for announcing the Muslim call to prayer and convert the inside into a mosque for worship.

The most well know example is the conversion of the Hagia Sophia church in Istanbul, Turkey, into a mosque in 1453. The church had been the world's largest cathedral for nearly a thousand years, standing as one of the great symbols of Christendom until the Ottoman's overran the church and converted it into a mosque on May 29, 1453. The great mosque stood in Istanbul as a symbol of the Islamic subjugation of Christianity for nearly five hundred years until 1931.

You can imagine the delight and euphoric celebrations when the fighting Muslims of the Islamic Empire get their hands-on Israel's glorious new temple. Their joy will be especially sweet since they reluctantly had to make room for it as part of the covenant with Israel on the Temple Mount. The invasion and subsequent capture of Israel's temple will be a bloody takeover and corresponds to the timing for the death of the Two Witnesses, Moses and Elijah. The celebrations over their deaths follow the common pattern of Muslim celebrations when high profile subjects are captured and killed.

> When they (two-witnesses) finish their testimony, the beast (Caliphate) that ascends out of the bottomless pit will make war against them, overcome them, and kill them.
>
> And those who dwell on the earth will rejoice over them, make merry, and send gifts to one another, because these two prophets tormented those who dwell on the earth.
>
> Revelation 11:7, 11

Like Israel's false prophets in the Old Testament who dishonestly told of a bright future in spite of the imminence of God's judgment (Jeremiah 6:14; 8:11; 14:13-14; Lamentations 2:14; Ezekiel 13:10, 16; Micah 3:5), so will Israel's political leaders blindly promote the false promises of peace and security in this future covenant with Antichrist.

> For when they shall say, PEACE AND SECURITY; then sudden destruction cometh upon them, as travail upon a woman with child; and they shall not escape.
>
> 1 Thessalonians 5:3

Chapter 12

WARS UNTIL THE SECOND COMING

THE FINAL 3.5 YEARS

The end will come like a flood: War will continue until the end, and desolations have been decreed.

> Daniel 9:26

And there shall be a time of trouble, such as never was since there was a nation, even to that time. And at that time your people shall be delivered, everyone found written in the book.

But thou, O Daniel, shut up the words and seal the book, even to the time of the end

> Daniel 12:1, 9

ABSOLUTE OR REGIONAL AUTHORITY

After establishing his headquarters on the Temple Mount, during the second half of the Tribulation, Antichrist will be caught up in a dramatic series of wars *"until the end."* Daniel's prophecy above makes it clear, however, that Antichrist's Jihad quests and his effort to conquer the whole world, to bring it under subjection of the Caliphate will fall short. Antichrist will never fully gain absolute world dominion.

A common misunderstanding today is that the kingdom of Antichrist will include every nation on earth and every person on earth. This is not taught in scripture. Antichrist's empire will be regional in the Middle East, not worldwide. As we have seen in this study so far, his empire begins with ten Middle Eastern Muslim nations. In this final chapter, we will look at the record of his attempts to expand his kingdom out from there.

The inaccuracy of those who suggest that Antichrist will control the whole world is seen when Daniel says there will be, *"wars until the end."* The "end" he's referring to is the end of the 7-year Tribulation. The clear meaning of this verse is there will be nations not in alliance or under the authority of Antichrist. Daniel 9:26 establishes the reality that right up to the end, Antichrist will be at war with other nations. Simply stated, a king with absolute, universal authority is not at war.

The presence of wars establish that Antichrist does not control every nation on the earth. Instead, we are told that wars will continue until the very end. The presence of wars prove the presence of resister militaries and thus resister governments and nations. If Antichrist had absolute authority over every nation throughout the earth, then he would also control their militaries. But that is not the case and is proof of Antichrist's limited authority.

MILITARY EXPANSIONS OF ANTICHRIST

Thus the common theory we hear that Antichrist will miraculously bring world peace and prosperity is unscriptural. He is a man of war (Jihad), worshipping Allah, the god of war (Daniel 11:38) and moving out to "conquer" (Rev. 6:2) the nations from the time he arrives until he is defeated at Armageddon.

The Bible primarily addresses his military expansions during the final three and a half years. That Antichrist will conquer many nations is very clear. But what is also clear is he will never conquer every nation.

Daniel 11:36-45 provides an overview concerning the military expansion of Antichrist's Kingdom. Twice, the passage says Antichrist will *"invade many countries"* (11:41-42). Egypt is mentioned as a nation that will fall to his forces (11:42-43). Beyond this, we are told Antichrist will invade the land of Israel, called, "the Beautiful Land" (11:45).

But this passage also reveals that "Edom, Moab and the leaders of Ammon" will escape from coming under his control.

> And he shall come into countries and shall overflow and pass through. He shall come into the glorious land. And tens of thousands shall fall, but these shall be delivered out of his hand: Edom and Moab and the main part of the Ammonites. He shall stretch out his hand against the countries, and the land of Egypt shall not escape.
>
> Daniel 11:40-42

It is noteworthy that this passage says many will fall, not "every nation will fall." And then, it lists three ancient kingdoms that will escape his hand. By grouping Edom, Moab and Ammon together, it is likely the passage is referring to the modern-day Kingdom of Jordan. Based on this passage, Jordan will not come under Antichrist's authority.

ANTICHRIST SEEMS INVINCIBLE

Just a few verses later, we learn that in the midst of his conquest, Antichrist hears of "news from the east and the north" which troubles him and throws him into a frantic state of rage and aggression.

The "news" is probably military intelligence reports about serious threats advancing toward the Caliphate.

> But rumors from the East and from the North will terrify him, and he will go out with great wrath to eliminate and annihilate many. And he will pitch the tents of his royal pavilion between the seas and the beautiful Holy Mountain; yet he will come to his end, and no one will help him.
>
> Daniel 11:44-45

We are not given the names of these invading forces, but they are significant enough to worry Antichrist, who heads out to confront them. Most likely, they are a unified front on their way to stop the madness of Antichrist's Jihad. There's good reason to believe that by now, the world's economy would be collapsed and the world's oil supply would be interrupted due to the eruption of non-stop wars from the Jihad campaign of the Caliphate.

Who are the invaders described as coming out of the East and the North? Since the context of the passage is dealing with the wars of Antichrist in the second half of the Tribulation, the invaders from the east here are not the same "kings of the east" referred to as coming in the battle of Armageddon (Rev. 16:12). Therefore, it is reasonable to suspect these are two large nations still able to function and resist Antichrist.

Commentators have suggested that China (in the east) and Russia (in the North) could be in mind in a final joint effort to stop Antichrist before the world collapses under the weight of his insanity.

FALLING SHORT OF RULING THE WORLD

What we can conclude from this text is that there will be nations in the earth not in alliance or under the authority of Antichrist. Right up until his end, Antichrist will be at war with "many nations."

Despite the fact that Antichrist's dominion will be limited, it is also clear that his military apparatus will be a force to be reckoned with. In Revelation 13, we see the peoples of the earth asking who is able to make war against the ferocious beast. It will seem as if none are capable of waging a successful war against him.

> And they worshiped the dragon, for he had given his authority to the beast, and they worshiped the beast, saying, Who is like the beast, and who can war against it?
>
> Revelation 13:4

Just like all previous kings who ruled mighty empires, when his time is up, the leader of the last and greatest empire in history will meet his end. At the height of his power, when he seems invincible, Antichrist will be defeated. There is One who can strike down Antichrist and *"war against"* the beast, and He's coming in the clouds of glory!

Then they will see the Son of Man coming in clouds
with great power and glory.

Mark 13:26

THE BEAST AND HIS ARMIES DEFEATED

The Second Coming of Jesus Christ is the capstone event
that will defeat Antichrist and bring his empire to an end.

Just as Antichrist will be revealed at God's appointed
time, after the rapture, when the restrainer is removed (2
Thess. 2:7), so also there is a divinely ordained moment for
his destruction. Antichrist's reign of terror is short-lived. Just
like his domain was limited in scope, his duration is limited in
time, to a period of 42 months or three and a half years (Rev.
13:5).

The final and most decisive battle for Antichrist and his
Caliphate armies is the massive thrust into Israel to annihilate
the Jewish people at the battle of Armageddon. It's a stunning
scene that's painted for us in Revelation 19:19.

And I saw the beast and the kings of the earth and their
armies, assembled to make war against Him who sat
on the horse, and against His army.

The deceptive powers of Satan are on display in this
scene. As the beast's great military forces are gathered by the
millions, they look heavenward and see the sky filled with their
arch-enemy-combatants of Jesus and His heavenly hosts. As
the Lord and his armies descend toward the Mount of Olives,
what do the kings of the earth do? In a final showdown of
rebellion, Antichrist's followers point their missiles into the
sky and start firing.

Of course, Jesus and His angels can neutralize those nuclear warheads in an instant. Revelation does not picture a long, drawn-out battle; instead, it is a battle that is over almost before it has begun.

> Then that lawless one will be revealed, whom the Lord will eliminate with the breath of His mouth and bring to an end by the appearance of His coming.

> 2 Thessalonians 2:8

> But the court will convene for judgment, and his dominion will be taken away, annihilated, and destroyed forever.

> Daniel 7:26

DOOM OF THE BEAST AND FALSE PROPHET

His followers held him to be invincible. They asked in the utmost confidence, *"Who is like unto the Beast? Who can war with him?"* (Rev. 13:3). But without striking a blow, and with all his armies around him, he is 'taken,' captured as a lion seizes his prey, dragged away from the field of battle, with millions looking on, as a helpless prisoner. With all his power and supremacy, he is 'taken.'

Accomplished with greater ease than the Jewish mob took Jesus, the "cloud-rider" on the white horse catches him away from the center of the greatest military force ever assembled. Any resistance is hopeless. He cannot help himself, and all his armies cannot help him. He's gathered up and tossed into the lake of fire.

> And the beast was seized, and with him the false prophet who performed the signs in his presence, by which he deceived those who had received the mark

of the beast and those who worshiped his image; these two were thrown alive into the lake of fire, which burns with brimstone.

Revelation 19:20

The beast's two demonically empowered leaders are yanked off the battlefield and dealt a crushing blow being thrown alive into the fire. The prophet Daniel saw Antichrist as boasting and always running his mouth, but his confidence has been stripped away in the presence of the King of kings.

Then I kept looking because of the sound of the boastful words which the horn was speaking; I kept looking until the beast was killed, and its body was destroyed and given to the burning fire.

Daniel 7:11

SOLITARY CONFINEMENT FOR 1000 YEARS

Revelation 19:20 is the first mention in Scripture of the lake of fire, the final hell and ultimate destination of Satan, his angels, and the unredeemed (Matt. 25:41).

Revelation 14:11 says of those who suffer there, "The smoke of their torment goes up forever and ever: they have no rest day or night."

Apparently, Antichrist and the False Prophet don't die but are transformed miraculously into their eternal bodies suited for their destination in the lake of fire. They are the first two humans placed in the lake of fire and remain there, by themselves, for 1000 years! A justified penalty!

As the two most evil, vile, blasphemous people who have ever lived, it is only fitting that these two be the first to arrive in that awful place. Their solitary confinement will end after the Millennial Kingdom when hell is emptied of its residents to join Antichrist and the False Prophet along with Satan and his angels for eternity (Rev. 20:10-15).

Bereft of their commanders, Antichrist's leaderless forces will then be destroyed by the Living Word.

> And the rest were killed with the sword which came from the mouth of Him who sat on the horse, and all the birds were filled with their flesh.
>
> Revelation 19:21

THE TRIUMPHANT RETURN OF JESUS

God is setting the stage for the glorious return of His Son, Jesus Christ, as the conquering King of kings. It will be a day unlike any other in human history when the sky lights up with the appearance of the Son. The many prophets who speak about this day fill in more of the details showing the scene of Christ's Second Coming to dispatch His enemies.

> Then the Lord will go forth and fight against those nations, as when He fights on a day of battle. Then the Lord, my God, will come, and all the holy ones with Him!
>
> Zechariah 14:4-5

> They will wage war against the Lamb, but the Lamb will triumph over them because he is Lord of lords and King of kings—and with him will be his called, chosen and faithful followers.
>
> Revelation 17:14

His radiance is like the sunlight; He has rays flashing from His hand, and the hiding of His might is there.

In indignation You marched through the earth; In anger You trampled the nations. You smashed the head of the house of evil to uncover him from foot to neck. You pierced with his own arrows the head of his leaders.

Habakkuk 3:4, 13

You will fall on the mountains of Israel, you and all your troops, and the peoples who are with you; I will give you as food to every kind of predatory bird and animal of the field.

Ezekiel 39:4

Now Enoch, the seventh from Adam, prophesied about these men also, saying, "Behold, the Lord comes with ten thousands of His saints, to execute judgment on all, to convict all who are ungodly among them of all their ungodly deeds which they have committed in an ungodly way, and of all the harsh things which ungodly sinners have spoken against Him."

Jude 1:7

And I saw heaven opened, and behold, a white horse, and He who sat on it is called Faithful and True, and in righteousness, He judges and wages war. His eyes are a flame of fire, and on His head are many crowns, and He has a name written on Him which no one knows except Himself. He is clothed with a robe dipped in blood, and His name is called The Word of God. And the armies which are in heaven, clothed in fine linen, white and clean, were following Him on white horses. From His mouth comes a sharp sword, so that with it He may strike down the nations, and He will rule them with a rod of iron; and He treads the wine press of the fierce wrath of God, the Almighty. And on His robe and on His thigh He has a name written: "KING OF KINGS, AND LORD OF LORDS."

Revelation 19:11-16

THE FINAL FATE OF THE EMPIRE

Jesus' adversaries at His coming will be the hardened sinners who thought their Mahdi was invincible and believed in the false god Allah.

They have defiled His judgments and scorned the gospel message sent to them during the Tribulation. During the final seven years, God has sent the preaching of the two witnesses (Rev. 11). He also raised up 144,000 special evangelists (Rev. 7, 14) and even sent a preaching angel (Rev. 14:6-7) to invite men to trust Christ as their savior.

Despite all the devastating judgments they will have experienced and the powerful gospel preaching they will have heard, they will stubbornly refuse to repent (Rev. 9:20-21; 16:9, 11). Since neither judgment nor preaching moves them to repent, Jesus will return to destroy them and send them to hell.

Jesus had previously warned mankind of the consequences of rejecting Him.

Repent, or else I will come to you quickly and will fight against them with the sword of My mouth.

Revelation 2:16

God's enemies will be killed by the decree of the Word of God, and their flesh picked over by the birds. The ill-fated battle will, in reality, be a slaughter. The Lord Jesus Christ will utterly destroy the beast's forces gathered against Him at His Second Coming. The Lord will effortlessly crush the greatest armed force ever assembled when He returns with the church and His holy angels to establish His kingdom.

God is a God of love and patience and grace, but His justice requires punishment, so those who destroyed the earth will be destroyed (Rev. 11:18), and in righteousness He judges and wages war (Rev. 19:11).

As we think back on the dramatic rise and immense popularity that Antichrist and his Caliphate achieved in the Islamic world, we are reminded of the brevity of life and how quickly events can change.

Antichrist first gained notoriety by striking a peace deal with Israel. Then he gained fame by stealing Israel's temple and setting himself in it as god (Mahdi). He grew in popularity for 42 months by blaspheming the Trinity from his Islamic Headquarters while briefly ruling from God's throne on the Temple Mount.

The world was awestruck by his military campaigns, saying no one could stop him (Rev. 13:4)! During his seemingly invincible reign, the empire of Antichrist had power and authority unparalleled in human history.

Then it will all be over.

Then the iron, the clay, the bronze, the silver, and the gold were crushed to pieces all at the same time, and they were like chaff from the summer threshing floors; and the wind carried them away so that not a trace of them was found. But the stone (Christ) that struck the statue (Caliphate) became a great mountain and filled the entire earth (Christ's Millennial Kingdom).

Daniel 2:35

ON THE END TIMES

Epilogue

Closer Than Ever Before

One day in the future, all this will come to pass. None of us knows when it will be. When Jesus comes again, there will be rejoicing and celebration for all his followers, yet it will be a time of judgment for all who are not.

If Jesus comes soon, which group will you be in? Celebrating in great joy? Or fearful of your future?

If you are a follower of Christ, God's Word regarding Jesus' return implies some urgency, encouraging us to share with others the Good News so that more will be ready.

If you are not a follower of Christ, may you open your heart and believe that Jesus paid for your sins on the cross and rose from the dead. May you seek the Lord and ask Him to forgive you of your sins and trust Christ by surrendering yourself to Him.

Salvation from sin and death only comes through trusting in Jesus Christ, the Son of God, as your Lord and Savior.

Let it be known to all of you and to all the people of Israel, that by the name of Jesus Christ the Nazarene, whom you crucified, whom God raised from the dead—by this name this man stands here before you. He is the STONE WHICH WAS REJECTED by you, THE BUILDERS, but WHICH BECAME THE CHIEF CORNERSTONE. And there is salvation in no one else; for there is no other name under heaven that has been given among mankind by which we must be saved. (Acts 4:10-12)

May you put your trust in Him, for Jesus is coming again. His coming again is closer than ever before. Today is the time to be ready!

FOCUS
ON THE END TIMES

CPSIA information can be obtained
at www.ICGtesting.com
Printed in the USA
LVHW050903140122
708387LV00014B/1103